CW01371542

THE GOLDEN DOT

ALSO BY GREGORY CORSO

The Vestal Lady on Brattle (1955)
Gasoline (1958)
The Happy Birthday of Death (1960)
The American Express (novel) (1961)
Long Live Man (1962)
Elegiac Feelings American (1970)
Herald of the Autochthonic Spirit (1981)
Mindfield: New and Selected Poems (1989)
An Accidental Autobiography: Selected Letters (2003)
The Whole Shot: Collected Interviews (2015)
Collected Plays (2021)

First page of book; all others pages
have no order,ergo a shuffle poem--corso

The mind goes round and round
the inspiration goes straight
thus the poem is beginning middle and endless
these poems have no ~~order~~ order
it needeth no binding
yet for sake of keeping poems together
read them at any page
It matters not what comes first or central or without end
it all goes round round round
like the lovely order of things
the gentle wise endless circle--

GREGORY CORSO

THE GOLDEN DOT

LAST POEMS 1997–2000

EDITED BY RAYMOND FOYE & GEORGE SCRIVANI

LITHIC PRESS
FRUITA, COLORADO

The Golden Dot
Copyright © 2022 Hillary Richard
All Rights Reserved
The Estate of Gregory Corso is administered by Sheri Langerman Baird, Executor.
ISBN 978-1-946-583-666

Cover Photo of Gregory Corso, May 3, 1986, New York City, by Allen Ginsberg. Courtesy Allen Ginsberg Estate

Frontis: Holograph manuscript from *The Golden Dot*, Courtesy Downtown Collection at the Fales Library, New York University

Back cover: Self Portrait, c 1990. Collection Zachary Wollard

**

Some of these poems appeared in *Cape Cod Review* (John Landry, editor); *Guest [a journal of guest editors]*, and *Castle Grayskull* (Micah Ballad and Garrett Caples, editors); *Gagosian Quarterly* (Alison McDonald and Wyatt Allgeier, editors); *–normal* (Enrique Juncosa, editor); *The Brooklyn Rail* (Anselm Berrigan, poetry editor).

"melted parchment," "Reluctant to sleep away this night," "the need is there," and "weird traces of light" were privately published in Athens by Raymond Foye in 2019 with Greek translations by Yannis Livadis.

LITHIC PRESS
fine books for an old planet

www.lithicpress.com

To
Roger and Irvyne Richards

CONTENTS

Introduction
by Raymond Foye
11

Editorial Note
by Raymond Foye & George Scrivani
19

The Golden Dot
21

Index of Titles and First Lines
173

INTRODUCTION
BY RAYMOND FOYE

> This is how it happened:
> At the end
> everything that was
> dwindled into a dot;
> the dot exploded into the void
> and the beginning began again—
>
> Gregory Corso, from *The Golden Dot*, 1997

Time, cosmic and terrestrial, was one of Gregory Corso's great subjects. He saw the decades as distinct parcels, the centuries as larger cycles, and millennia more so. Throughout the 1990s he had been eagerly awaiting the arrival of the millennium, exploring in his poems themes of Armageddon and apocalypse, ecological cataclysm, Revelations, and the promise of a New Age. But as the momentous date approached, personal tragedies mounted: the death of his closest friend and literary champion, Allen Ginsberg, in the spring of 1997, followed four months later by the death of William Burroughs, the person he considered most incorruptible in life. In 1998 his oldest friend Anton Rosenberg, model for Kerouac's hero in *The Subterraneans* (and "the true hipster" in this book), passed away. Then came news of liver, heart, and lung disease, and finally inoperable prostate cancer. He managed to see the new millennium, but only just. He left his beloved Greenwich Village for the care of his daughter's home in Minnesota in 2000, and died shortly thereafter, on January 17, 2001.

Corso had struggled with his final manuscript, *The Golden Dot*, for the last twenty years of his life. It went through countless visions and revisions, both textual and conceptual. He knew it would be his poetical last will and testament. It had to be precisely on the mark, a summation of the many literary and philosophical themes that preoccupied him in life. Even more daunting than the personal hardships (which were nothing new to him), he had changed his fundamental approach to the poem, casting off an elaborate stylistic toolkit that no longer served his purposes. The rudiments of the poem were what mattered now, a direct and elemental relationship with the Muse. Frustratingly, throughout the 1990s, the project continually collapsed under its own weight, until...

Following Ginsberg's funeral at New York's Shambhala Meditation Center, Corso returned to his small apartment at 26 Horatio Street in the West Village and composed "Elegium Catullus/Corso, for Allen Ginsberg." It is modeled on a funeral ode by the Latin poet Catullus, who sits next to and addresses the "unspeaking ashes" (alloquerer cinerem) of his brother. Corso lightens Catullus's famous final line, *Ave atque vale* (Hail and farewell), with the salutation he and Ginsberg always used on each other, "Toodle-loo"—a bit of '50s camp silliness they often shared. With this short and simple poem, the floodgates opened. Over the next 3 1/2 years Corso reconceived the entire manuscript of *The Golden Dot*, beginning that evening with the "Elegium."

The Golden Dot is framed by Ginsberg's death on one end and Corso's own death on the other. It is, among other things, the story of a lifelong friendship between two of the great poets of the twentieth century. Corso is now alone, left to argue with his mentor and rival, pleading his case and making amends. His insecurities lead him to question the very reasons Allen befriended him in a Greenwich Village bar: was it just his good looks and street smarts? But he comes to trust and accept Allen's estimation of his work, so succinctly stated on the dedication page to *Reality Sandwiches* (1963), some of the only serious recognition he ever got for his poetry in his lifetime: "Dedicated to the Pure Imaginary POET Gregory Corso," and once again in Ginsberg's *Selected Poems 1947–1995*: "To Gregorio Nunzio Corso, Wisdom Maestro, American Genius of Antique and Modern Idiom, Father Poet of Concision." Allen always told anyone who would listen that Gregory was the greater poet, and often lamented the lack of serious critical studies of Corso's work.

Corso did not like to overpublish, and by the 1960s one book per decade became his general rule, usually at the turn of the decade, with each book expressing something of what he felt to be the zeitgeist of the moment: *The Happy Birthday of Death* in 1960; *Elegiac Feelings American* in 1970; *Herald of the Autochthonic Spirit* in 1981. Another rule was that the books should be brief: these were 92, 120, and 66 pages respectively. But by the time 1990 arrived, Corso chose not to publish. He turned sixty that year, and while his reasons for not publishing were never clearly stated, profound changes were taking place in his life and work since "Hitting the Big 5-0," as he called it in a poem marking his half-century. Corso's relationship to poetry had been a trajectory from intensely private to famously public, sometimes reading to audiences of a thousand or more. He complained to me often, "I began writing poetry alone, after midnight, just me and the poem, by candlelight. The next thing I know I'm on stage reading to hundreds of people. It messed me up." This predicament led Corso to favor humorous poems, crowd pleasers with punchlines. He'd come to see himself as a performer, a clown, even, in his own words. He had been on the reading circuit for twenty-five years, often touring with Ginsberg—they were public poets in a way that is almost unimaginable today, and they both took that role very seriously. But Corso's brash persona and drunken antics at readings masked a painful shyness, and he longed to escape that grind. As he so memorably put it in a poem of the time, "I feel like an old mangy bull crashing through the red rag of an alcoholic day." He'd come to see this public face of poetry as a routine, a job, an act. And while he may have had many shortcomings, failing to be honest with himself was not one. Slowly he withdrew, first to Rome (where he always felt most at home) and then to the neighborhood where he was born and raised, Greenwich Village.

These had been hard years. The drinking itself was no longer sustainable and that necessitated a separation from society. More profoundly, the half-century mark awoke in him the need to confront the many traumas that haunted his adult life: abandonment by his mother shortly after his birth due to domestic abuse by his father; five cruel Catholic foster homes, four orphanages, and seven arrests, with frequent prison time in the Tombs. The orphanages and prisons had always been part of his personal mythology, but until this point the painful details had never been publicly examined or revealed. And once that door was opened in his writing, it could not be closed. Sharing these details with his readers makes for an unprecedented intimacy, one that could never be revealed in public readings.

Corso was a native New Yorker, born on the corner of Bleecker and MacDougal Streets. Gangsters frequented the cafés and restaurants and the culture of organized crime was hard to resist. From individual acts of petty theft, Corso eventually became the ringleader of his own larceny gang, whom he organized with walkie-talkies. At the age of seventeen he was sentenced to three years in upstate New York's brutal Clinton Correctional Facility, known as Dannemora. Ever the prodigy, he often noted that he was the youngest inmate to enter that prison, and the youngest to leave.

There's a remarkable film of Corso on a return visit to Dannemora Prison (as he always called it) two years before his death, speaking with prisoners about writing poetry. He recounts the advice an old inmate gave him the day he arrived: "Don't serve time, make time serve you." The prison library held few books but they were choice: *The 1905 Webster's Illustrated Dictionary of the English Language*, the *Bible*, the *Encyclopedia Britannica* (eleventh edition), *Bulfinch's Mythology*, and a 1925 anthology titled *Ideas and Forms in English and American Literature*, edited by Homer Watt and James Munn. I recently obtained a copy of the latter for a few dollars, after finding Corso's reference to the book in the manuscript of *The Golden Dot*. It's a fascinating selection and explains a great deal about his penchants for early epics such as *Beowulf* and *Sir Gawain and the Green Knight*, and for the ballads of the British Isles, such as "The Twa Sisters" and "Sir Patrick Spens." Running through all of Corso's work is a healthy mistrust of literacy and the written word, which he considered latecomers to his profession. The stories and beliefs handed down orally from ancient times were his true guides, and he always said his favorite author was Anonymous. He loved Sanskrit and Akkadian epics, chronicles of dynastic Egypt, the myths of ancient Greece. His sense of history was synchronous: ideas, events, and subjects all connected inside his head like the gears of a clock.

I first encountered Gregory Corso in April 1973 at a Jack Kerouac symposium at Salem State College in Massachusetts, where he was a featured guest along with Ginsberg and Peter Orlovsky. That weekend, with velvet suit and silver flask of cognac, Corso was on the attack against everyone: Ginsberg, the academics, and Kerouac himself, or at least the myth of Kerouac. (The witches of Salem seemed to be the only people he had any respect for.) But then something remarkable happened: the event concluded with an evening poetry reading, and I saw Corso take all of the hostility he had created and suddenly polarize it. (Later I would see performers like Nina Simone and Miles Davis do the same thing.) After ninety minutes of poetry and chanting by Ginsberg and Orlovsky, Corso took center stage and read what I still consider to be his greatest poem, "Elegiac Feelings American (for the Dear Memory of John L. Kerouac)." Suddenly a hushed silence fell on the auditorium as Corso cast his spell; the poem was profound, eloquent, and ravishingly beautiful. At the end of the reading, many in the audience (including many Kerouac family members) were weeping, as was Corso himself. There was no question who the heavy was on that stage.

One of my favorite things about hanging out with Gregory over the years was watching how he dealt with fans. He had a lot of them, and since he always looked like Gregory Corso, they often approached him on the street. Depending on his mood he might be gracious, but was more often flatly dismissive or downright confrontational, accusing them of pandering and vicariousness—*they* were the source of his pain. "Mister Corso, I just want to say how much your work has meant to me down through the years," someone would say in a heartfelt manner. "Do I bother you with my problems?" he would reply curtly. Other times he was more practical: "Oh that's great, gimme $5." I can't count the number of people who came up to him to say that his poem "Marriage" was read at their wedding—a true epithalamium for our times if there ever was one. (The poem is heavily anthologized; Gregory once told me he estimated he'd made over $100,000 from "Marriage"—"Not bad for one poem.") Especially surprising to me was the number of people who quoted back to him the line "Standing on a street corner doing nothing is power." Written in 1953, that line somehow represented the quintessentially Beat challenge to authority. And as Gregory often said, one great line is worth an entire book of poems.

Corso did not reveal his inner nature casually. Those who met him once or twice only saw a theatrical personality. For this reason the many outrageous stories that abound may be accurate in their picaresque details, but they are also terribly superficial. Underneath it all he was a figure of great warmth and caring, as his closest friends will attest. It seems strange even to me, but when I look back on my life most of the truly important pointers I got—about human nature, self-preservation, and other life lessons—came from Gregory.

Whether Gregory was home alone, playing pool in a bar, or sitting in a cafe, there was never a time when he wasn't *with* the poem, turning a line or image over in his head, speaking it aloud to test the sound and cadence, or questioning the inner logic. He loved the aporia—the philosophical conundrum—and this book is replete with them; he puzzles over ancient riddles, and offers new ones of his own. The intent is to bring the reader to a place where they don't know where they are. His poetry was an argument with himself. I never knew anyone who worked harder than he did, although if you asked most people they would probably say he never worked at all. A scholarly issue was always on the table, and he was familiar with them all. In a barroom one afternoon he suddenly slammed the table with his fist and shouted, "It was all because of that damned swan!"—and I knew he was back onto the Trojan War.

*   *   *

In 1997, his sixty-seventh year, as he labored over his final book, startling news arrived. A documentary filmmaker discovered his eighty-four-year-old mother: she had not returned to Italy immediately after his birth, as he had been told, but had merely fled across the river to Trenton, New Jersey, where she raised another family. Their reunion was captured on film, and a few days later they made their first excursion, to an Atlantic City gambling casino—which seemed to establish matrilineal proof beyond doubt. But joking aside, though initially joyous, the reunion only re-exposed painful feelings of abandonment. Corso told me a few years later that he wished the filmmaker had left well enough alone. "I lived sixty-seven years without a mother—how can all that be made up for now?" (He always claimed Demeter to be his true mother.) Meanwhile, his father was dying. Corso had hated and feared the man all his life, but he made the effort to visit him, only to find that Alzheimer's disease had turned his father into a gentle and kindhearted soul. They had a poignant reunion, but the encounter ended on a painful and embarrassing note: his father called him Dominic. These and other remarkable tales are recorded in *The Golden Dot*. Life now seemed a daily succession of bewildering events.

One positive development in these years was the emergence of a patron, Hiro Yamagata, a successful visual artist from Japan. His monthly stipend allowed Corso to move out of the apartment of Roger and Irvyne Richards, proprietors of the Rare Book Room on Greenwich Avenue, who had taken him in several years earlier after he'd spent the night on the subway. When an apartment came vacant next door, Corso had his own living space for the first time in many years (or practically ever). There's no doubt this helped with the work. Those of us who visited him will recall the floor covered in typed poems, often stained with wine, coffee, blood, and god knows what else. The space also allowed him to begin making art again, which brought in a little money. He was a skilled draftsman with a charming style and a deep knowledge of art history. He had his visitors and admirers and a calm domesticity prevailed. The one vexation was his addiction. A heroin user since the 1950s, now alternating with methadone, he told me it had been almost twenty years since he'd actually gotten high from the drug—it was simply a matter of maintenance. Veins had collapsed and he was losing use of both arms. Infections led to visits to nearby St. Luke's Hospital. He recounts these events in several poems, always referring to heroin as "the dirty nurse."

Corso often spent years revising a poem, and in many respects a poem of his was never finished. Friends who gave him lodging would later find his books in their libraries extensively rewritten. Poetry readings, especially in later years, often consisted of glosses on the poems; he always seemed to be having a running argument with himself, or the poem (they were the same thing). But as the end drew near he seems to have realized these endless revisions would not do, and suddenly we have the rarest of things in his oeuvre: poems written all at once, a single stream of thought and inspiration from start to finish. This is sometimes indicated to the reader by the date of composition, and often even the exact time (always in the middle of the night). Corso called these "diary poems" and he was extremely unsure about them. To me they are the capstones of his career, the works that most show off his extraordinary powers as a poet. To read a poem such as "melted parchment" (dated 4/26/98) is to fully enter his mind, and to witness the very act of the poem's coming into being. In these last poems he has gone back to the candle, at midnight, writing to himself and the solitary reader. For much of his life, poetry was connected in his mind with youth: not only the teenage spirit of Chatterton or Rimbaud, but the child spirit prior to that. Keeping that spirit alive had a lot to do with how he lived, and it took its toll. Now wisdom and old age come to the fore. The level of intimacy is exquisite and the effect ethereal. The conviction he had for the poem was absolute.

Another unusual characteristic of *The Golden Dot* is how very few poems have titles—perhaps only half a dozen out of a hundred or more. I don't know why this is, except clearly titles were superfluous. One is left with the sense that these are not literary "products" but a kind of unnameable issuance or outflow. It also facilitates Corso's wish, stated on the first page of the manuscript, that this work be seen as a "shuffle poem," with a random, nonhierarchical configuration, or, if one were more occult-minded, a method of divination like the shuffling of the tarot or the throwing of the I Ching. Such a book as this may exist somewhere, but I know of none like it.

The reader may ask, if this book was completed twenty years ago, why is it only being published now? After the poet's death the apartment was cleared out and the manuscript was gathered into a paper shopping bag. In his will, Corso left the rights to the book to his friends Roger and Irvyne Richards, for their faithful support in his final years. Roger Richards, a legendary figure in New York's rare-book world, died at home on his seventieth birthday, December 18, 2002. In less than two years, Irvyne had lost her two closest companions in life, and she gradually became a recluse. I called numerous times, hoping to obtain a copy of the manuscript, but she always demurred, saying she wanted to edit the book herself—which I knew would never happen. Irvyne was a chain smoker and for years I lived in fear the apartment would burn down and the manuscript with it. Eventually she stopped taking my calls. The original work remained in her possession, a talisman to a life that no longer existed, and she guarded it against the outside world. When I learned of her death, in September 2020, I called her stepdaughter Hillary and soon the manuscript was in hand. Although pages had been copied and circulated among Corso's friends over the years, those were clearly fragments and drafts, and bore almost no resemblance to the carefully shaped final manuscript, with the author's intentions everywhere evident, the concluding chapter of a profound career.

In 2021, this book was rejected by both of Gregory Corso's lifelong publishers, New Directions and City Lights. With his publisher friends James Laughlin and Lawrence Ferlinghetti also departed, Corso was once more the orphan, this time in a world he helped create. I am grateful to Danny Rosen and Kyle Harvey at Lithic Press for making this work available to old friends and new readers.

EDITORIAL NOTE

As a working manuscript, *The Golden Dot* has existed in many versions since the early 1980s, some of which have circulated in private hands. In these versions Corso explored such disparate topics as the murder of John Lennon, the Branch Davidian massacre in Waco, Texas, and the racial injustice of the Port Chicago disaster of 1944. At times the manuscript contained extensive autobiographical writings, and Corso usually included as centerpiece his longest poem to date, *The Day After Humankind,* an imaginative romp that takes place the day after the nuclear extinction of the human race. None of these poems, nor many other fine examples, appear in this book. The poet himself turned away from this material as he narrowed his focus to his final subject.

The typescript we are working from is a very specific one that Corso composed between 1997 and 2000, the story and focus of which is recounted in the *Introduction* to this volume. This typescript is now in the Fales Library at NYU and may be examined there by scholars and interested readers. In our opinion this last typescript was not a finished work, in the sense that Corso was never able to prepare the book for publication, always an intense editorial process of winnowing that the poet approached with utter ruthlessness, usually in marathon sessions in his publisher's offices as the deadline loomed. By far the greatest challenge we faced in this project was this reckoning. Given that together we shared many decades serving in various roles as Corso's literary friend, helper, editor, typist, translator, and/or publisher—we had to rely on this experience to guide us in our decisions about what to include and what to leave out. In no instance did we interfere with the individual poems.

In assembling this edition we have chosen to preserve aberrant spellings, antique grammar, and coinages that were unique to the poet's style. The designation [...] indicates a torn manuscript page where lines are missing. We have recognized that the rawness of Corso's manuscript is an inherent part of this book. We have avoided the impulse to add footnotes, believing such annotations would be an intrusion on the text. The place names, historical and mythological figures, etc., found in these poems are easily researchable, given today's wide availability of reference information via the internet. Lesser-known friends of Corso's mentioned in passing in this book include Francis "Duke" Sedgwick (father of actress Edie Sedgwick), and Hope Savage, Corso's first girlfriend and muse, and subject of Deborah Baker's fine study *A Blue Hand: The Beats in India* (2008). One now dated but key reference is the name Sinclair in the poem "There were two times…"

(p. 110). The Sinclair Oil Corporation was famous for its gas stations with their tall revolving sign featuring a green dinosaur.

A note about the book title: for many years the working title of this book was *The Golden Dot*. In keeping with his ever-reductive impulses, Corso later shortened it to *The Dot*. A few years later it became simply: *Dot*. Then, in a final subversive stroke, he titled it simply: • A point in space, the big bang, the black hole; and as Corso sometimes explained, what you see when you take a line and turn it on its end. It would be a title unique in literature, and one that would be a permanent headache to publishers, librarians, writers, et cetera. With a certain regret we have returned to the poet's original title, while feeling obligated (and not a little guilty) to share this background information.

Although we have tried to realize what we consider to be the truest intentions of the author, it is our hope that this volume will inspire other editors to examine the wealth of materials that exist in the many private collections and research libraries, and that future scholars and editors will make their own contributions to the posthumous career of this difficult and delightful poet, who wrote much but published little.

We would like to express our gratitude to Gregory Corso's family for their enthusiastic support of this (and other projects): Sheri Langerman Baird, Lisa Brinker, Belle Carpenter, Cybelle Carpenter, Max Corso, Nile Corso, Kaye McDonough, Sally Schubert, and Miranda Schubert.

Raymond Foye & George Scrivani
New York & San Francisco, 2022

THE GOLDEN DOT

*first page of book; all other pages
have no order, ergo a shuffle poem—corso*

The mind goes round and round
the inspiration goes straight
thus the poem is beginning middle and endless
these poems have no order
it needeth no binding
yet for sake of keeping poems together
read them at any page
it matters not what comes first or central or without end
it all goes round round round
like the lovely order of things
the gentle wise endless circle—

Elegium Catullus/Corso

for Allen Ginsberg

Every night of our youth
was One last gaudy night
in and out many palships,
admonishments:
Don't drink, screw up poetry readings
I am sitting buddha-style by your coffin of gold
my yiddishe grandma, here I am
for this final parting
to bestow at last these words which the dead are given
to eulogize
and mourn in vain your unspeaking ashes
since rigid Fortune forbids you to hear me or answer
O my blessed brother so abruptly taken
I celebrate my grief with funeral tributes
offered the dead in the ancient way of your choice
accept these words, wet with my brotherly tears, and
now and forever, my brother,
as your last words were to me on the phone
I return to you
toodle loo!

"weird traces of light..."

weird traces of light like inverted shadows
disc the air where my fingers picked something up
& boomerang where my elbow dropped itself
could be tired as the time could tell
though i have kept these hours long & lively
for reasons lonely & vain
mostly sad like the fat woman trying to fit in her dress
we are both attempting beautiful conversation in our minds
& i wonder how long it lasts
we question it w/ all the right answers, forever?
I am sick at the thought of catching up w/ them
like they were right all along
everyone exactly the same & entirely content
why is it so binding?
why are the silken strings stretched about me so?
if you are so inclined, cut yourself
& tell me if your pain is identical
go ahead & stuff the gash w/ linen
be a mary magdalene redeemed
the eyes will kindle the atmosphere
spacey sounds your eyes perceive audibly
headaches & whoredoms clothed in christ
that was no trap door
nor false panel
my distortion is honest as a drum
i am sorry for the changing graces they give us
absolutely brokenhearted that she doesn't stand near me
her skirt was patchwork like my quilt
in an hour or less i'll be underneath
remembering she slept on my bed once
imagining things differently until
it all bends like memory into another day

3/22/98 4:07 am

"I am frighteningly lost in the present…"

I am frighteningly lost in the present
I cannot hurry from the house
and go see my dearest friend
—he died not long ago
There's my mother
she's vowed to care for me
but I don't know her
After 67 years of life
I've finally met her
—she lives far away in New Jersey
I don't know what to do in the street
where to go…
People, life—all different
I hardly know anyone
The old hangouts, some gone, others: strangers

I cry sometimes for my dead friends
sometimes for no reason
I feel wracked with guilt
guilt for some unknown sin
perhaps never committed
It wasn't so much I failed my friends
but myself
It was only later by harsh realization
that these friends were god-blessed
After a loveless life
these angels without wings loved me
Ignorant of love, confused,
I was not aware of my destiny
Did God command: "Go, go love the unloved one"

It took a year
and the many deaths during that year
to end the life I was long accustomed to—

This new life
bereft of all things familiar
seems as though I had died
and then came right back to life
to a world unknown to me—

"This is an autobio…"

This is an autobio
I suggest you read
In one sitting how poetry
first came to me—
In time you'll notice
I'm duadic; I've voices two
They're easy to distinguish
My profile at left is unlike the one at right
I feel I've an encyclopediac
as well as prophetic Janusian mask
beneath my face
The face I see and all else see
is the true mask—
No one knows the Janus beneath
People believe the mask covers the face
yet impossible it is for them to unmask that mask of flesh
It is Janus brings the glow to your face
You can't confide with Janus in the mirror
the way my dear Buddhist friend advises
Sayeth he, Meditate, say hi! to your face
regard your eyes, whisper: Janus…O Janus….

"I was born 1930…"

I was born 1930
It is now 1997
I am 67
I was born a poet
An orphan since birth
I lived alone
The foster homes I was shipped out to
kept me in single locked rooms
My friends were crayons and paper
and my imagination
I wrote my first poem
never having heard the word poetry
I was my best friend
I wrote to myself
mostly my dreams
and imaginings

I read my first book
a gangster book
in the Tombs age 13

I lived on the streets until 15
I spent 6 months in Windsor Prison, VT
read *Les Miserables* there

Spent three months free
and was sent back to prison
Clinton at Dannemora
Plattsburgh, New York,
for 2 ½ to 3 years…
there I read all the books I could get my hands on
and endlessly wrote to myself
It really wasn't myself I was writing to
it was the world; I was writing to the world
—that's why I called them poems
and had them published—

"And because the cause of it…"

And because the cause of it
had to do with Faith and Knowledge
I put on the self-brakes
realizing I was in my years
and to see if I was mentally responsible—

Not of my making
but I sense I'm accountable…
By thought alone
cemented in logos
one's able to tip the balance…
what proof the imbalance?
Right or wrong must one press down?

   Change
   there's always change
   and no change in itself is change

I know what was my crime
but now
what is my crime now?
Hubris, it has to do with hubris—

Who has the choice
to prepare for remission?
The chances of living are 2 to 1 against me
I am a doctor of heart idiosyncrasies
I know the body can destroy malignancy
My heart is an ongoing mystery
Pull out the cannons!
I'm either gonna kill myself or kill the ill
All's spontaneous remission with me
I'll never know why I get well
and believe me I'm a mess—

"I've become a recluse…"

I've become a recluse
I don't go out
I sit
Don't walk
Take cabs
Seldom eat
Maybe a plate of veggies
Three times a week
Lots of puddings and pies
I am without woman
That's why I'm at a loss to care for myself
What angels women are

The phone rang
insistently

It was that guy who always
tells you shockers, like plane crashes

dead friends or celebs: It was Princess Di
I told him thanks, gotta go back to the tub
…went back to the machine and lay back…
Seems her death hit England or the world
like JFK's—
Strange, but for Shakespeare
I love the famous English dead, young—
What I don't like is the cruelty peopled-life bestows—

It wasn't me
I dug deep down
They were sitting by the fire
They saw me asleep on the couch
They were proof it wasn't me
I was up to my elbow

I finally had something solid
I yanked it up
I took a deep breath
What is it? they cried
How did I know? I was asleep on the couch

"I have near a decade of poems..."

I have near a decade of poems
I'm prepared to volume—
After LONG LIVE HUMANKIND
I published at the end of the decade
Elegiac Feelings American
Ten years later I bestowed an unsaleable title
on the lovers of poetry:
HERALD OF THE AUTOCHTHONIC SPIRIT
Dopey people who rumored I lost America's greatest
publisher of poetry, New Directions,
err'd, alas, err'd—
The ten years are up—tho I was once told
Poetry is the property of youth—
Lost of religion since 13—53 years later, today
may I create and benefit the life we're fated to live
—pray the divine powers that be to ease the insufferability
and pain that endlessly lessens the fleshed xerox of God.

"It sneaks up on you…"

It sneaks up on you
Things are left uneaten
What falls is left where it fell
I wake up and that night sleep
in same unmade bed
Upon a quilt blanket of down
Another quilt of down covers a most comfortable night of sleep
The phone rings I answer it not
My doorbell rings…I return no answering ring
I force myself to carry down the garbage daily
a person of the street, an inmate amongst others
I enjoy living alone, a becoming recluse
I swore off the drink now that I've ceased reading aloud
poems to an audience of strangers…the pain to read what
no longer pains me…truly shy, I'd get drunk and feel
no pain; I am unable to read aloud what was written from
the soul's very depth—I learned to read the poems that caused
    laughter…
I prayed the day I'd be read as I read Keats, Clare, Vaughn—
Now that I have given up reading in public
I delve into the depth of the soul and tear it apart
that I surgeon-like cut out the horrid ill
brought down to us ancestrally
by the expelled one, he rightfully is by form and name
the Great Con—eat, he told them, and you'll know
all your Master knows—In truth they found what the snake
knew, which was slight—Confounded Faith with Intelligence
They, like the snake, were expelled

Old friend, regard my hands
they seem Egyptian; mummified—
I am too tired to connect with my children;
about a year ago I had energy enough
It came asudden; like when overnight my hair turned white

Today at age 66 I wonder if I'll see my 70th year
A mere 4 years…and I have my doubts!
A decade earlier age 56 I was facing year 2000, 14 years hence
I could outlive a cat in that amount of years; they'd 8 extra
But 4 years, you ain't gonna outlive no cat—
My oldest friend, poetry, and a close second old friend,
the poet Allen, has passed the 4, he being 4 years older than
me—Chemicals; Kerouac and I agreed dexies kept us awake;
but prose is remembrance and lots of detail;
when i wrote nigh ten years of notebooks, scraps of paper
speed had me complete the work of 10 years in a month or less
—I paid big. Speed had me crash hard; the only panacea
was heroin. The poems were long since done—typing was the final
draft—I'd augment; I'd delete.

"In time anger wrought of vengeance…"

In time anger wrought of vengeance cools off and all is forgiven

No:
In time vengeance wrought by anger

bides generations like a swollen-eyed snake unforgettable: natural—
forgiving

"reluctant to sleep away this night…"

reluctant to sleep away this night
only because i did that last night
and woke up worse off—

my voice almost logical
sounds like coffee & cigarettes
straining for a Dylan Thomas "drone"

needlessly rocking
back & forth in fetal luxury

lullaby time i'm sure

it will be sorrowful
the last strands of life breaking

then its over
& beginning
something formless new

no more legacy of a benign cancer

i'll return to unborn listless bliss
sleeping the sublime lathe of an ignorant fetus

or rising phoenix-like from pandora's box
of breathing cinders & breeding ash

swooping down on a nectarine bowl
broken-
but tonight

reluctant as i am
i'll suck the nectar succulent from solitude's teat

the stranded connection won't split
for some time I think
i'm glad

for the motion of my body
somehow cradled
armless as I am

4/11/98

"I have nothing to say…"

I have nothing to say
nor wish to say anything
To cease pondering where
the talk circuit resides
I become a Russian revolutionary
and storm the brain
and dash up an ornate gold-gilded swirl of stairs
A long hall to my left had a trembling door
Only the shake of fear
like nervous rats
dare be so stupidly ostentatious
Better confront the fearful than the fearsome

AAAAA – on the page

to write what in/or out of time
is destined to become obscure
a confoundability with no measure of incomprehensibility
each and every word existing in each and every verse
arouses one to hail as one would galaxies apart
his use of proximity between two obtuse words—
A poem published in an all but non-existent
8th issue of a college magazine
may say a century hence resurrect a poet
who's equal in poetry; though he's one to show for it;
one poem, that is; be none other than Andrew Marvell.
Indeed our newly discovered poet will ponder
"Has Marvell written more than 'To His Coy Mistress'"?
A good match indeed; both one poem poets!
Were Marvell not secretary to one far greater than he, Milton
he might well have writ more;
but the one out of print great poem;
what mattered it had it never been found—
To have written such a poem, surely he knew himself;
and felt what God in creation, felt—
Vermeer without doubt felt and knew;
same goes for me brother poet, Allen; and, hit and miss, me;
I felt the act of creation almost a debauch;
and knew who I was wholly ignorant of poesy,
so it was the gift came to me—
The only living poet who defined me sure was Allen:
For the pure imaginary poet

"What I want to know…"

What I want to know
no one can tell me

They're dead

Alive one of them
used to call me
always wanting to know
"How are you holding up?"
I used to tell him
my mistake
I learned too late
In no time all the culture-vultures knew
how I was "holding up".
About a year before his death
I'd answer all his "Are you all rights"
with "Fine, Al, fine, couldn't feel better"
I'd asked him: "It's my heart; no more salt, fats,
"I'm on a rigid diet…" I'd be crying
I never told a soul; my oldest friend in life, he was—
He meant me no harm, he figured people would feel for me
if he told them I was unwell.
I just didn't like people knowing my friendship calls.
It was always his heart. A year later he was told
he had five months the most, he died two days later
And it wasn't his heart!
Those damned doctors! It was never his heart!
It was his liver; cancer and hepatitis C of the liver
They, the doctors, finally found out 2 days before he died.

The other caller was his gatekeeper
Through him you'd get to a man I loved
and knew it for years
It was okay, the phone
was not an instrument to talk to my Wilhem to—

"The old chemicals carried my labors…"

The old chemicals carried my labors, at times,
seven sleepless nights; I was young and no worse
for it—
My heart 30 years later murmurs, is tired;
I can only labor the most 4 sleepless days—
My appetite is gone;
yet I've no other workable option—
Creation had nothing to do with it;
the poems were written the decade past—
Creating was never labor;
tailoring the work of 10 years
was work, putting my trust in a tired heart;
bereft of appetite; I could say:
My life is on the line—
Ah blessed humor, I am laughing,
what if the work done ends up the stuff
of desperation…spirit abandoned; and a mind
become ill?

"Penguins and bears…"

Penguins and bears may tear up my sofa chairs
and seals roll on my bed like eels in a barrel of oil
If it gets too cold boil cans of snow and sing Hi-ho!

If eskimos come tapping on your igloo
tell them to take their seal meat stink and go—
I don't need this arctic crap, what with furriers traps
and footless sables who ate their own feet to free themselves
…disgusting, and this cluttered cabin of mine
I never knew to get up and clean up;
it's all a mess! seal skins, bloody polar
teeth piled high until I make necklaces of them;
but how, I gotta drill holes in the teeth;
I aint got no drill! I shoulda stayed home;
the good thing is: I don't wish I were dead—

"From birth to '80 no one I knew died..."

From birth to '80 no one I knew died
Kerouac, an aberration—
From 1980 to 1998 relentless!
They were dropping like angels (can't say flies)
No one is hardly left
My nearess dearess oldest friends in life:
Bill B; Allen G; Anton R; Herbert H;
All gone…in a matter of one year—

I have not lived a healthful life…perhaps good genes
I was younger than all of them, but only by a few years
There's no poet friend for me anymore
All the poets I honor are dead

the only poet I know and have
is myself
This book, these poems, are a constant flow
Redundant, Chaotic, profoundly heart-felt;
without order, just as my days, my years, my health;
illnesses – All poems are one; each poem is all;
start from the end, or middle, or beginning,
indeed, the shebang is endless—
It's the work of 10 years—

Yes, put your hands to your ears
and demand your inner stentorian heart
be still… such accursed voices seldom adhere
The soothing hands of incestuous flesh
is the only remedy…yet was more cowardice than guilt
prevented him indulge
How he yearned for the guiltlessness of Paganism!

I'm no longer in trouble
I mean, I handle things
before it's too late;

if I wait, trouble comes
For no reason I put myself in trouble;
give myself worries;
while all the while I've enough
problems like an enlarged heart;
asthma; lack of potassium; poor eyesight;
like I'm a mess!
I just don't know how to care for myself—
Women know how to
but I don't chase women anymore—
All my friends are dead
and those related to me
are better off without me—
I still have my poetry
I thank the powers that be for that
God bless—

"There's one thing you'll never get from me…"

There's one thing you'll never get from me
My heart has always lain bare
I have things that embarrass me
Yet I'm uncaring about them
I'm an opened book
Except for that one page
That I tore out and burned long ago
I'm due to die in the near by
Most my friends are all gone
I just don't feel it will serve any purpose
Letting go of that one thing I know
I should keep at least one thing to myself
And why be so hubrisian to think
That it'll be of matter to anyone anyway?

"when god is me…"

when god is me
and not me he

who culls my spirit
leaving my labors undone
awaiting that rare visit
from the Hidden One

He loved youth
who told me Poetry
is the property of youth

Euripides, Sophocles,
wrote great works past their 90s

tell me properly now
no "I was only kidding stuff"
let it out…all out
I know somethings couldn't be helped
you had no choice
to escape pain is excusable
don't suffer it
anyone in your position
would have done the same thing
the heroic man, numb to pain, sweat and blood
the tongue lopping sideways from the dry mouth
the speechless eyes, glassy unto death
you are not that man
no one is
except him

"I believe people are born…"

I believe people are born
with the choice they chose to be
I was born a poet
because I wrote a poem
never having heard the word POETRY
As a child raised in houses without books
living in closed rooms
my only companions were color pencils and paper
I'd draw
and write what I felt in short lines
When I reached prison (the Tombs) at 13
a man wheeled books around
and wanting to learn English good
I got a book on rhetoric
—in it I saw my first poem
or the short lined kind I used to write
in those lonely foster homes as a kid
I'm good proof of two things
One, you can be born a poet
Two, when you're alone poetry
can be your best friend—

"Ask me not of moons…"

Ask me not of moons
unless you can hand me Jupiter on a salver
It's a matter of size and gravity
Earth, one moon, fittingly so;
Jupiter, my god the size of it!
7 moons; figures, eh what?

If you wish it
you can tell me about Alpha Centauri;
(Proxima Centauri) I guess that planet
as well as Beta Centauri, are planets
that belong to our closest galaxy
Andromeda…You know it:
It's an angled spiral with two big stars by it—
I don't care how big and plentiful
the megagalaxy is, the entire cosmos;
it's still finite—
In the Absolute all that isn't is infinite—
There's always more of that which isn't
than that which is—

It will come what came before
Though nothing of it shall return
Replacements of the masters are masked
The Anti ones are the true ones
Beware the mask beneath the face
Smiles have nothing to do with sincerity
Sincerity is a most untrustworthy word—
Like: What are you sincere about?

Hope fills the flagon of the Future
The Celt Man Of Years drank his fill

The torc'd man was Dorian man
His was Greece & Magna Græcia

Etruria man was Eastern man
His was Rome; Britannia was his return home

Time passes in its arrival
Anchored to the Present

Space expands in its departure
Vacuuming the Past with anticipation

"Closing a file drawer..."

Closing a file drawer
with a strained hand
got while stepping in a street hole
which sent me flying
and coming down
landed on said hand

It pained something awful!
And at a most inopportune time too:
I was on my way to prison,
Dannemora Prison,
oldest in New York State,
where I first entered 50 years ago—

At his death
a few scattered flurries

Paris
I'm returning
My beloved city
Nothing of sight changes there
The people...ah, the people;
that's the only sadness about it all,
the people, my people, are gone—
I'll walk amongst new people
reminiscing about past people—

Dear Hadriano, I was drunk
...so what else is new?
I'll tell you:
Your pretty boy Antinous
came to me in a dream
wreathed in Nilotic reed
his young lovely face
fish-nibbled   in no manner different
than time's wondrous play on ruinous marble

"How can I convince you…"

How can I convince you
I'm not a bad man
No one has to convince anyone
about one's self
But there's something about me
isn't sure about me—

I look into the mirror
eyes to eyes
and couldn't see me

I was always shy of myself
I'd get embarrassed for another's embarrassment
If I was given a compliment
I'd return it with a weak smile

I just don't know me…yet—

Then it happened…I got to know a me
Drink brought that me to me
A demon if ever there was—
I'd get up and face thousands of strange faces
and recite from the depths poems laid bare
Tipsy I dare only read poems that brought laughter
Never would I venture poems from the dark night of the soul
So I became a clown…how I wept for beloved poesy—

"I have grown up, haven't I?"

I have grown up, haven't I?
I mean I'm 67
That's grown up, isn't it?
Of course it is.

I remember being afraid
I was 15 on a subway train
I looked at the old people
Surely, I assured myself,
I'll be mature like them someday
That's when I became scared
"What if I remain like I am?" I asked myself
"What if I don't grow up?"
I felt so faint
I got off immediately at the next stop
I couldn't breathe
"Was I Dying?"
I left the station
I didn't know where I was
But the air felt good
I realized that night I didn't know anything
Raised Catholic why didn't I ask Christ for help?
I wish I knew people like those I met later on—

Believe it or not I'm shy
The thought of getting up on stage
and read my most private inner feelings
to an audience I believe hates me
urges me to get plastered
and most of the time I can't hold my mud
For the life of me I read only light funny poems
get them laughing then run
Comes the morn like most drunks I moan

"O my god what happened last night!"
I acted more grown up as a youngster
than I have as an elder—
Like I said, that was my greatest fear—

"It was always old people told me…."

It was always old people told me:

As long as you got your health—

Two things happened to me overnight:

Teens began calling me "pops"
and my hair turned white overnight—

When I was with step-parents I was told:

"Good Riddance Bad Rubbish"; "A lost cause";
"I should have dumped you down the toilet bowl"—

"Is love instinctive…"

Is love instinctive
Is it a gift from whom we're born
Motherless, can love be taught
Who loves the abandoned child
Who loves the unloved
Hard it is to love
To be loved
What more insufferable than
love lost
Love oft God's alias
To love not another is piteously painful
To love not one's self is reverse hubris

I loved things romantic
Most things I loved
seemed lifeless
I loved beautiful marble Greek statues
I loved young dead great poets
I loved the lands of the Past
Sumer, Egypt, Greece, Rome, Israel,
the unprobed Orient—
I loved the mythical gods
I have gained something
I opened up to Faith
Faith in what?
I cannot say
But it's a thing alive
a thing I can feel
I have Faith in the human condition
Faith I have that death is not the end of all
This Faith so recently gained
so endlessly denying in the past
I would an inch of knowledge
than an infinity of Faith in that which I have no knowledge

Nay, I say to you it takes Faith to gain knowing
For without Faith I am without spirit

   A nothingness
   olding…olding fast
   Was only yesterday the good people in life have died
   I am alone

   I must rise
   I must
   for soon the time of getting up shall have passed

"What I don't know…"

What I don't know
I know well

The finite is the pit
of the infinite

When it came
it wasn't something asked for
It was more a gift
anonymous—

When it ceased coming
there was no way getting it back
I was sure the giver was no Indian-giver
I looked to myself, the obvious fuck-up—

        I took what was given

"O tell me nice man…"

O tell me nice man
    who sees my pain
 are my dead and dying friends
    making life insufferable?

Of course not
I'm the one
not phoning
not a letter to anyone
Not getting in touch with my kids is inexcusable
I don't eat
Really have no appetite
I'm at an age
that when I was younger
most my friends were older
that's why now they're dead and dying
I don't go out
Gave up poetry readings
There are rare times
I jump up
and go somewhere
do something
I haven't loved a woman nigh 10 years
Unhealthy; it's…no,
I can't say that, it's over
It's not in me
I'm not like that
True, I may well be a hubrisian creep
It hurts feeling unloved
It could be all untrue
I love my wives and children
I know I'm not totally a loser
I have Faith
In what, I'm asked?
In the human condition, in Hope, Love

"I first entered the Tombs…"

I first entered the Tombs
when it and I were brand new
It was the time of toilet bowls
and electric light
The residents of the old Tombs
told me about the place:
Wooden buckets of piss and shit
and kerosene lamps—
They ate where they relieved themselves
Animals the same; natural for them;
in time it becomes natural for humankind…
it's a matter of morality or something,
I mean people make love, lick each other everywhere;
taste pee, shit, come, who's kidding who…?

Anyway I first entered the Tombs
age 12, then 13, then 14, 15, 16
months at a time…all for petty theft;
all because I couldn't raise 500 dollars bail—

That's where I wrote poetry
Where there was none—
No books; never the word "poetry" spoken
12 years old I knew to sing
from birth to 10
I lived alone
in a dark room
my only friend me
I imagined
I found the key
Everything unlocked with imagination
Blame me for loving Greek Myths
more than Liver-eating Johnson, Davy Crockett,
the myths of my heritage, America?

"And when last told…"

And when last told
I obeyed

After 67 years
from the womb which bore me
"I am she
"You shall live with me"

I've lived alone most of my life
Though she was my mother
Our blood was strangers

Tell me O great poet ne'er born
if the meaty bard with melodic breath
lessens the song that might have been
am I full of suppositions or what?
For instance, did Emily D., have to be?
Of course!

The world will end year 2012
…thus states a Mayan codex

Now that my life is complete:
Having seen the mother I never saw
She a strong delicate 84
I at 67 blessed with good genes
I've seen more than most people have seen of life
The changes, the risings, fallings…

It'll always come back
the good, the wrong, you've done
Life is truly so precious
the memories of the past
always return to remind one of mistakes
mistakes that shame one of life's frailties
teaches one to think, go slow, respect the sacred moment

the importance of it all
the goodness of it
it means being saved, means going to heaven
life O life
truly it's something, don't know, can't say

"prepare for a dismissal of sorts…"

prepare for a dismissal of sorts
missaled & hymned
through all my books
& personal phantom pages
coffee stained
herbal eyed
me—
fallow for the new thing
I am pushed far enough
coldly striped enough
nails long
beard be song
never knew the ease of the end
like this could be
enough of a gag to all along smoke
cinder stint—
blighted eyes gagged
      struck
      forty
      lashes
      save
      one

3/30/98

THE DAY MY FATHER DIED

He was 88 and had Alzheimer's
I saw him two years ago
he sang an Italian song, kissed me,
and called me Dominick
He was a horror to live with
I spent the most 2 years with him
He served on the battleship New York
and I served years in prison
I was raised by foster mothers for 8 years
When he married the Rabbi's daughter
I went back to live with them
He converted to Judaism
Raised in a Jewish neighborhood
I knew the WWII sorrow of Jews—
He died today
and being Jewish he gets buried tomorrow
I couldn't make it; not enough time—

His cemetery was in San Antonio, Texas
I'm unhappy not making it, but I am joyed
to have made up with him, even tho he called me Dominick

"A man gets older…"

A man gets older
he can become age wise
who'd argue with that?
Does what I said have someone biting their nails?
Has a call gone out to the bullpen?

It makes no difference
relevant or irrelevant
I sat down to poem a poem
An idea of gravity
—a thought from years ago returned
The sky is not only up but down
Some thought
Maybe had it 30 years ago
Upon becoming age wise
I heard the music of fallen things endlessly falling
My brain fell the equivalent of 3 g's on the Cyclone
What thrills poetry rewards!
I say to poetry: God Bless

You can tell when a poem doesn't make it
Simple: You don't make it
The reward, the thrill, orgasm, no come—
Strange…creation
then miscarriage
Spiritless
making it without the Muse
…just fucking masturbation

"Before the upper side of the twirl…"

Before the upper side of the twirl
one sparking line came straight down
then curved into demonic mouths
which spoke diamond-sized sounds

Seen was heard
and like a map in twirl a sea was heard

Whirl spiraled whale eyes
see and hear going down and up for air;
say an ocean became a desert in a squid's blink—
Heard and seen became conglomed
and all walked the earth, then what happened?
Mammal returned home coming up for breaths of surface;
perhaps a day they'll all return home
—evolution takes no known time; it hath no kalend—

The dinosaur was here the day before I was here
Time was measured the instant I was born;
It took 4.8 evolutional years before my clock began

Wasn't La Brea tar pits
stopped the clock on the sabre-tooth & giant sloth—
It had to do with food…when fern and other tree eats
climately died, the oils, lubricants, had the giant
saurians suffer the death of constipation—
Could be before the tar pits became pits
they were oceans of oil drowning all
then in climatic time buried them in deserts of sand—

Better to see and hear
than be seen and heard
Safer to be weak than strong
safer to be thought the fool than the smart-ass

To twirl on ice with ice-green eyes awhirl;
like a Scandia Druid have a snowwoman
enwrapped in evergreen; abound in afreets
with hair of ice cycles

The devil's hourglass rests in every climate
of the earth; – Greece: shades—Assyria: dust & clay
—Britainer: fog & damp—Numeria: sun & lion's breath
Norway: snow & ice—Libya: desert & sand-storm…

"This brain a half century ago..."

This brain a half century ago
sets down in poetry how it was set forth then:
Gave thought without thought
I'd use a word because of its beauty
Words like: CYPRESS, IONIC, EPHEMERAL,
I'd write fast but not incorrectly;
the syntax lucid;

the hits and misses;
the corny rhymes;
ate her/later; any obsolete, archaic, word would do—
spontaneity; likes: like this, like that etc—

"Written at the hour of my death
"I commend you, my furry ball of love,
"to statuary, i.e., cold marble
"that the eyes of days coming
"may gaze upon such as I have had to
"during 18 years of wedded arctica"—

"There it was sitting across from me…"

There it was sitting across from me
on the edge of the bed
its feet never touching the floor
I never questioned it; just stared at it;
that's all, just stared—

Whose room it was I had no idea
Must have belonged to it
because as an orphan
I never had my own room—

Nor did it speak to me,
it sat there, like me;
staring, saying nothing—

It has hands, eyes, a face,
body, and all, don't know about brain;
I mean I can dangle a puppet before it,
its eyes follow, but doesn't reach out—
Someday I'll speak, but I see no ears;
maybe it plays on vibrations—

Everything it wears is green;
One day I dangled a green thing at it
…behold! It grabbed it—
It didn't give it back; instead it ate it—

Songs hit hard as icy snowballs
Big dreams are living proof of broken hearts
Love and survival run through hospital halls
like blithe departures of death marking the charts

In time the face you'll get all at once
shall example the Talmud's sibylline words of old
—Not until your 40th year of wisdom shall the dunce
flip off his cap and see the face ere its mold

"I feel like writing a beautiful poem..."

I feel like writing a beautiful poem
A smart, Shakespeare-smart poem
I have that fine knowing feeling
I have the power
The kind my dead poet friends no longer have
They were great poets
All the great ones are the dead ones

The Mermaid Tavern sign squeaks
like a mouse caught in a windy creaky door
each squeak lets go a dot of blood on the hinge
Within the velvet suits have a boot up on the bar rail
"Brightness falls from the air" was your best
And "Fat as butter; cheap as an egg" yours
Back and forth it went
Each poet reciting the other's best line

When am I gonna realize I'm too old for this
I don't go after it
It's offered
I take
Pure Russian Roulette

So far I'm still alive
So I take pity on myself

What is this?
All my poetic life
I've been finking on myself!

"I love you as I love my fear..."

I love you as I love my fear
that young oak outside
and baby cat
mocking me
The creeps!
They know they'll outlive me
I could play devious
…stunt that tree
get the horny cat
I know a nymphy feline
it'd be a catastrophic disgusting premeditated old meany thing
to do—
I make monstrous faces at little babies in carriages
Smug little truncated Churchills!
Yes, you've a life to come
and me one to go
but let me tell you
you'll never have as many lovebirds in the sack
like I was blessed to have lived in the 60's
the Golden Age of my lifetime…
Dear Oak, favorite of trees;
I doubt my life would have floated so God ordained
without the wise love; knowing stare
in-drawn claws pawing my body as known to all
when life becomes too much; how brave we are,
and the great mystic understanding the generational
offspring of the Goddess Bast,—
braves life with us down the eons;
If the putty cat can endure life, pain and all—
who could think to close a life when
our furry little friends claim to hang around another 8

"I dreamed what might have been my first dream..."

I dreamed what might have been my first dream
A place I came upon wide awake
It was when I visited Olympia Greece 30 years later
I remember the shack of Phidias the sculptor
the furry caterpillars crawling all over
the sculpted blocks ready for Apollo's temple

I had to be three to have dreamt that
because there was a back yard, with a shack,
and a fig tree covered in tar paper
Strange, I don't recall any caterpillars—

My two companions weren't in the dream
They enjoined me in the reality return
One was the Indian son of a newspaper editor
and the other his lovely wife who Francis Bacon
did nightmarish paintings of
She never forgave me when one mischievous night in Mycenae
I hid behind the twin headless lions
the entrance gate
and as they were walking towards hidden me
I jumped out and sang Ta-la!
She screamed, grabbed her heart, and has hated me ever since;
not her husband, he was a poet
and introduced me to Edith and Osbert—

Speaking of Ms Sitwell
profiled like Dante
she invited myself and Orlovsky
Orlovsky with Allen in tow
to a fancy ladies club
she called it the Lady Macbeth Society
and we all ate watercress sandwiches there

"Who can deny when a truth becomes redundant…"

Who can deny when a truth becomes redundant
the propaganda of it brands it cliché?

A truth told is ever recalled
The mind lacks memory of a lie

A thing never remembered
is a thing non-existent

There's something about being set free
I speak the release of all; armageddon—

Each death is armageddon to that death
Were all dead but one it'd be not armageddon

Armageddon is when no one is alive to know thus
Your death alone shall not undertake the death of the world

They sleigh up to the aether lands
with merrying hands fingering petals of flora
Then crash-dive across the Egyptian sands
winging Ka's and Ba's across starry Nut O implorer
the Ibis has landed on the Sphinx's head
with its speedy eyes the Pyramid Texts are read

Grab not that wishes not to be grabbed
Order not the brute to get below and work the bellows
None asked to come aboard who was nabbed
Those whose throats now bleed were once fine fellows
Now they stink of mummy cloth and dried worms
Whatever the parentage these were not of God's terms—

O How by temper and spared of anger you passed
the murderer's pit; yet to damn the damned
and suffer him his crime, you sooted angels
who by mere fortune could well have been you; indeed is
you! the dead are long dead;
yesterday is gone…gone

"Who was it…"

Who was it
I?
Six or so
years old
without a solid notion
of what made me do
what I did?
I started the day
the only way I knew
I stopped at that house
the one between home and school
What made me always enter that house?
It was in the basement
There were a pile of the latest comic books
and a plate of cakes with icing.

"Say when my time is up…"

Say when my time is up
Will I be welcomed at the Mermaid Tavern?
There's Joyce standing at the bar
with a booted foot on the brass rail
It looks like a haughty eye he's on me

It doesn't look good
There's Keats seated alone
looking dejectedly down upon his death mask
The bartender was standing at the far end
it was Andrew Marvell and he was conversing with Milton
There was Auden; him I knew
I acknowledged him
He smiled…or was it a grimace?
I moved away from the door
and began looking at the Blakes on the walls
Everything spoken was in whispers
I wondered what it took to get the digital axe here
86, that is

In walked a sturdy happy Whitman
He whispered in my ear "My vote got you in
"That shit Poe had a fit, I tell you"

I had learned it had nothing to do with poetry
whether it was major or minor
The important thing was
one's belief in oneself as poet
and experiencing the blessed feeling of creation
I knew the difference between
the abortions and creations
The feeling of creation is unforgettable

and…rare
I was given at birth
a gift or task

My ancestral background
goes back to Pythagoras and the Pythoness

Pythagoras, the first philosoph
had a school in Crotona, Calabria,
Magna Græcia: Greater Greece;
could be one of my ancestors
attended his school—

The Pythoness: the Delphic Oracle
while prophesying thru the ages
was paid in land;
she obtained that land, Magna Græcia
when Rome conquered Greece
One big change occurred:
in Delphi the Oracle had to be female
in Greater Greece now Italy
whatever sex the Oracle gave birth to
became destined to sit on the tripod
—in time a male sat on it and prophesied

"Two funny things I worried about in life…"

Two funny things I worried about in life
First: I wanted to be a better poet than Southey
Next: I wanted to be a better person than Nixon
What low goals!
An orphan, a ward of the State, pretty low on self-esteem
this lovelack boy now a man
Imagine wanting to prove my worth
on the backs of those two strangers
(Imagine I was going to write: On the backs
of those two sad men)
As I learned the truth about FAITH
So shall I get a handle on hubris…
I am double the age of Christ; Alexander
…all I need is that 4 years to hit the millennium.
Finally I've received my second chance—

Not the many 2nd chances of strangers, judges;
the guards of the State; the friends who were never my friends—
Unloved I never knew to love
I got my love from cats; I loved them so…
yet I gave them away; I even abandoned one…
Monstrous! I doubt Nixon was guilty of that!
I don't know if it's my Catholicism
this guilt business but it's about time I be done with it—
One last thing: If I abandon a thing that loves me
who the hell am I to cry orphanry—?
O God am I tackling hubris? Am I?
This awful painful reality! O dreams, my nurses, I am ill….

"Can one talk behind one's back…"

Can one talk behind one's back
though he be dead?

It was like the Manchurian Candidate
Alive I'd write he was like a brother to me
That if it wasn't for him I'd be dead
I came damn nigh close
to crediting him with my sole possession: Poetry
Why?
When we met was I
had my prison poems
He read them
Told me he was a poet
He loved me
Loved my poems
Ignorant of love
never experiencing it since birth
To credit him with my only joy I knew
I believed honoring him thus
was the truest sign of one's love for another—
Was mostly untrue
We were great poet friends
I got him to delve into Shelley
He got me to regard the musical language of
Hopkins; Crane, the divinity of Whitman…
My truest teacher was Hope, a young angel
I had met; from her I realized Mozart, Wagner, Bach—
Mythology, the Greek of Gilbert Murray;
the Chinese of Wang-Wei; Shelley bonded us—

"You never told me about Poe…"

You never told me about Poe
You told me about Whitman
I told you about Poe; Shelley—
When you laid Crane on me
I told you the two great ones
Poe & Whitman, killed him
—made him into an accordion
Poe was in, Whitman out;
in & out, in & out;
inward; outward;
enough to make one jump ship—

no need to call the dark aside
and whisper the natural badness of things;
the light will give testimony to it

downing pleasures with earth racing upward
the heart thumping thoughts of college days
with friends each wearing cool J Press ties
throwing snowballs with wild flows of hair
ruddy-skinned youth ever ready to frap
how beautiful the offspring of the sons of God
and daughters of men!

Merlin, silver-plated, oaken-skinned,
carried nothing too far
His shack, the floor covered with sheep skin,
had shelves, and on these shelves were jars
and in these jars were Martian tidbits
so their label stated—
Unlike Walt Whitman, he had no piles of yellowing
press clippings—
When Wilde visited Walt in Camden
drinking elderberry wine
"I like that Oscar!" exclaimed Walt
after Wilde had left;
was Wilde mentioned the old man's press clippings—

Anyway Merlin…he knew never to put a curse on someone
         with both hands
he always kept one free
so if chance willed it
he could always take the curse back with his free hand—
Mordred is that kid in a man Burroughs always
had contempt for
and he, Bill, suffered no fools;
yet was the fool plucked Excalibur
His name Percival, if memory serves me right;
I'm confused if it were he who sought
or obtained Holy Grail; was Galahad Percival?
Percival Parsifal? My eyes are bad,
and my encyclopedia is the tinniest of words—

"How to lose fear…"

How to lose fear
nameless, gut-curdling fear?
To claim something was done in the name of fear
is a confusion of mind; fear is nameless
…a deep breathtaking feeling; undefinable—

Was fear created God…primal man gained of consciousness
was so afeared of what those bleak damp days made him feel
he created a limit and called it God—

"Forces of Nature that destroy man..."

Forces of Nature that destroy man
Avalanches, tornadoes, hurricane, earthquakes;
frenzied fire, squalls, el niño, cyclones—
novas, supernovas, black holes, quasars;
cosmos, mega-cosmos, all that exists in outer space,
are but finite—
All that opposes this finity is infinite;
there is more that is not than what is—
were the cosmos megagalactic wholly,
there'd be no room for expansion,
and the universe is ever expanding

My friends who have recently died
in dreams I see again

I know they will witness the foul air, the scum waters,
the toxic air — earth ill, moribund, dead,
left to rot; the place of repair, burned down—
the rottage in time and sloth
will leave the blue globe dusty like a mummy;
volcanoes will vomit no longer but excrete—
The Mediterranean will return to the Mediterranean Basin;
The great savannahs of the Pacific and Atlantic—
Gone the whale, larger than any dinosaur—
Gone human kind, the lemur too—
Then as before in the great infinite void
a finite dot of life shall explode

Don't ever ever tell me
"get with it"
I, your eye opener—

Keep your eye dead center;
breathe my breath
I gave you a fire
you've yet to understand—

That's why you're all dying
after years of berating me as a know-nothing
at long last you learned I knew too damned well—
It's frightening, I held my hands in prayer up to you!
The smart lumpen took your words
and you died on the donkey herds—

"the dark night of the soul…"

the dark night of the soul
is seen with only your eyes
To record the sight in the word
illuminates all the darkness
that so insuffers the human condition
Nothing can be told humankind
that they don't already know
…the poet merely enlightens
the knowledge in the darkness of us all

There are nemeses surrounding poetry:
Hubris; arrogance; judgement;
the mockery of ignorance;
sloth; belief in flattery; fame;
the poem: a tool to deny God,
freedom to say anything shocking;
best way to get even with life;
with the values of society;
a most dangerous art: poetry—

"When the year 1 arrived for the descendants..."

When the year 1 arrived for the descendants
of those ancestors who had no conception
of the kalend;
timelessness was lived by the measure
of the spatial span
The megagalaxy grandest of all space
is finite—
That which exists not in the Absolute
is infinite—i.e., all that exists is finite;
all that does not exist is infinite—
Which is simpler: All you have is less
than all I have—
all galaxies in all its abundance is finite
the voidian emptiness in its Absolute is infinite—
Again, because all that is isn't
whereas all that isn't is i.e.,
what you have is finite;
what you haven't is infinite—

the labor is in dwindling the redundancy;
the finite-infinite thing can make it in a line or two—
To tailor the brown velvet suit when I enter the Mermaid Tavern
with Joyce and Allen seated at a table; and the Immortal Bard
a booted foot on the brass rail; I'll order a stout and vow
my soul to keep my mouth shut the entire stay—

the illness of fear he suffers only a few specialists
exist in the whole world, mostly Bangladesh
Their walls are filled with diplomas from colleges
that once existed when his grandfather lived—
This trembling shaky king of fear with pop eyes
told the specialist Your country has made me sicker

the above is an example; the garbage that clogs the brain
once released nothing of a saving grace exists therein—

A poem of one verse purifies the garbage;
the diamond in the rough;
poetry comes seldom and chance, it cannot be ripped off;
for Poetry is a sacred business; in the beginning…
the Word is age-old—without time, is there an end?
Was there a beginning?
Her egg is a spiked wheel and his sperm is like a tadpole
I witnessed thru a great machine reject those almost made it
ones then in no time entered the egg the one of her choice

that love children felt for each other
was so painful a pleasure when apart
I wish my life and wife's life that childhood love
we shared and hope to feel eternally

When beauty exists within
and the monstrous hovers near
the love that resides within
shall orb the proximity of the monstrous which exists without

"You 13 have your classical sources…"

You 13 have your classical sources
You are angry instability
mostly written black
you're a disquieting number for some
and you're a superstition not to be laughed at
Half a world away a door sealed with a waxen 13 on it
was discovered in the Gobi by a bandit named No-Noe Wu
he broke the seal and found behind the unsealed door
a suitcase and tripod
At that moment he forswore banditry and became a
    merchant
He set up the tripod, put the suitcase atop it, opened it
and began the first street corner; with all the trinkets
in the suitcase for sale; in time others followed suit;
in no time the city of Ulan Bator became the Capital
of Mongolia—13 is a number of good fortune as well—

I'll spin the tender roots of ravagement
like a bully a porcupine to rally their iron hair
then at sea-bottom ballet-wave with tubes and worms
and get tanked up with bloated coral fluids
Then have your head drain like blown bloodstains
jellyfish and climbing veins of a palsied crevice
in which the gaping mouth of the eel sways—

The endless fathoms of the lake
is two balls of string attached

"No, don't give me that…"

No, don't give me that
Stop; I'm hip to it all…
Young, you're immortal;
Now the old of your youth are dead; are dying—
From birth to ten maybe a grandparent pops off
From ten to fifty maybe a couple of accidents,
illnesses, nothing en mass—
But then cometh the big 5 – 0
Those twenty and over are dying like flies
Sometimes three or more a month go bye-bye
Old friends, a little older, same age,
even younger, die; are on their death beds—

Tell not the whip when it's the hand what hears
The shirt-torn back sun-wetted awaits the sting
of the coming snap—
Whipping and the amount of blows are not marked in law;
the duty is not to kill; it be a punishment meted out
to fit the offense, though at times
by no defined intent a soul might die of shock—

Well, they've made up their minds
they're going after the gold
It took them long enough to decide—

Oh they ride like men all right
upright, at even gallop, rifle steady on knee
but there's a sense of fear pervading them
perhaps it's because they're getting older
I don't know; it's all there, just for the taking;
what's holding them back?

"Had you but loved the lesser love more…"

Had you but loved the lesser love more
The nausea of lovelack would rack you less
When all's sucked in like the pull of a black hole
What can escape from the emptiness you feel?

The other side of the universe
is like the other side of the moon
Full of black matter
What is a quasar but the pin point
of a black hole

What comes out of the other end of a black hole?
A quasar, har har—

In my lifetime have I eaten more apples than pears?
Have I spent more on movies or drugs?
Have I had more sex than all my ancestors?

At your service
I lost my teeth in the service
I'm willing to undertake the death of the cosmos
I gulp everything like a black hole
And excrete what I ate at the end of the funnel
Quasars—

Be there a black hole in our Milky Way
Then in space-time we'll all be eaten up
and become the quasars born at the beginning
and have long ago died
We are dead—

Stringy black matter
vibrates in the void
in the ever-expanding universe
there is less to fill it absolute
For matter is less than anti-matter—

"Ah, Micheline..."

Ah, Micheline
it finally got to an unexpected one
Allen, Bill, your beloved Kerouac
my Anton, your Kaufman, Huncke
and so many others—
You died of natural causes
I was told today;
that you died today on
a train from Frisco
You were funny
Called all poets and painters
who made it: Sell-outs!
Was it because you never made it?
I thought you made it
There you were
in tradition of the bohemians of old
The famous have all sold-out!
And the time you told me:
"I'm done with poetry; it's getting me nowhere
"To painting, that's where I'm going!"
And cute Sesame Street pastels they were

Ah, Jack Silver
our time is going
The ship is sinking
Just two days ago the true hipster Anton died
I knew him since 1950
He introduced me to my great angel-love
Sura aka Hope
You, you were an acquaintance
Kerouac was kinder to you than I
I thought your poetry sucked
Forgive me…nobodys poetry sucks—

"I know where all the beauties are…"

I know where all the beauties are
Just look down, it's at your feet,
it's up ahead; across the street—

I'll let you in on something;
There is more what isn't than what is

And another thing:
There's nothing I can tell you you don't already know
Else how could you understand what I'm saying?
All I'm doing is illuminating what's already in your head

After they put economic form in place
Piggy banks shall smile upon
the sleeping babes of God…
The deficits their fathers accrued
shall have the monetary field leveled
and those once smiled upon babes
will skateboard the Miltonic highway in the sky
with the Son of Light still brooding at the edge
Both spiritual and cosmic inflation shall boom asunder
The ever-expanding shall join the deflation of black matter
Black Holes shall excrete Quasars
from the wide part to cone to pinpoint of its end—

Had I but cupped the bright winged bug
later than sooner
the soft amber would have hardened
and a fine trophy would my fingers have had
—instead in the heat of noon
the amber swallowed bug
flattened into a medallion of fried insect
of awful deformity

I still have to face
what all the great souls I love
who have lived before me

as well as all those great ones I knew
and loved no less
I still have to go through what they went through
Death

I weep not for the dead
I weep for the living
Myself
They passed the bar—

When we cry for the dead
we cry for ourselves
The only shot for me out of all this is
Whether they loved me or no
they'll be spared their tears for me—

"You cannot replicate the soul…"

You cannot replicate the soul
Though Blake wrote the profound simplicity
Like no two fingerprints matching
No way to rip off Blake
Indeed
Consider Donne
"Who cleft the devil's foot"?
Consider Emily D:
I taste a liquor never brewed
…not all the vats upon the Rhine
can yield such an alcohol—

One cannot replicate the gift
Sneak the miracle
A copy of the Mona Lisa
is just that

"When in dream I flagellate…"

When in dream I flagellate
with vinegared straw
from arm to arm
ranting mea culpa mea culpa
a sweaty burlap monk

I wake up in tux and top hat,
twirling cane and tapping Astaire shoes

I have no address
I expected no mail

There was a monastery
on the MGM lot
maybe they had a message or something;
also on the studio lot where Ginger and Fred
were working on a picture;
maybe something awaited me there…

Entered the monkage
to the very room I flayed my flesh
yet like a matinee idol with tux and top hat

A gargoyle from the set of Notre Dame
wailed to me: Why wasn't I made of flesh like thee?

on my way to the dance studio
I passed a plane hangar I had seen
in a dream dreamt years ago;
same hangar, same dream

"When something of power dies…"

When something of power dies
it dies in the living
Micro-sightings show an illness
and soon the power of life
becomes moribund

Never heard of an interloper
in the sperm run
Though I was told there was one
and it won
beat all them millions
got right into the egg!
Seems two guys got off into her
weird, no?

There were so many other places to be
than the ones I was at
Yet it always seemed I was at the right place?
at the right time—
The girls I met could have been other girls I met
The friends I had were rare
the kind that everybody wanted to be friends with
I don't think I could have met any others
different than the ones I met
Chalk it up to fate I guess

My lips took but never gave
Again I take back all I took
Love never given though banked
is never saved
Starved of love leaves one fat with emptiness
Just as the fat of pregnancy
all is but bloated water
Exiled from the womb
the separation greeted by a slap not a kiss

"I insisted on Beauty…"

I insisted on Beauty
when inspired

I obeyed
yet what flowed forth wasn't beautiful—

I aimed blame
like darts toward a dartboad:
I got bulls-eye on hubris—

Denial makes for a shaky hand
It was Faith
rather the lack of it
had me aim & connect off the board—

Knowledge without Faith is an imbalanced dart
Faith keeps the feathers straight
Its dart gains the eye perfect
The wisdom learned hits the mark—

"My leadership ability..."

My leadership ability
has never been exercised
like my ability to sing
Though Italian I was tone deaf
…yet I could cut my own hair fairly well

One whose parentage came from Calabria
they were known as "testa dura" hard-heads,
obstinate, stubborn, dumb like a donkey
yet that hard bare land held the likes of Pythagoras,
the Delphic Oracle, Magna Græcia…older greater Greece—

It's like the confusion on the word God
A man says he's God; I say he's confused—
A man says God is me; I say yes, he's right—
I can only be me
I can't be you, the tree, the sky, etc;
but God can be me, you, the tree, the sky, etc—
How sweetly beautiful the simplicity of understanding

I hold the highest respect for the best of all religions
Impossible for me to embrace the entirety of one religion
I love like a box of wondrous toys the Greek gods of yore
And the men of religion I honor are Jesus, Buddha…

"If I had strolled down the Via Sacra..."

If I had strolled down the Via Sacra
with my arm around Augustus' shoulder
knowing what I know now
I would have warned him to wash the figs he picked
for he wouldn't eat anything from any other hand
plucking the figs was the safe right thing to do
His wife knew this so she simply basted poison
on the yet to be plucked figs—
Claudius I would have warned too had I the chance—
Caligula, no, no way—

What's so mysterious about Eleusis?
I can tell you—
Though no one ever revealed the Eleusinian Mysteries
It's not too difficult to understand what the cult,
the initiation was about...
Of the three big Gods, Zeus, Poseidon, Hades,
there are multiple temples to Zeus, Poseidon;
but only one the third one, Hades, had one temple...
the temple of Death, Pluto;
therein lies the secret, the unrevealed, the mystery of death—

Demeter (whom I always deemed my mother)
had a daughter, Persephone, Spring—
Springday she strolled the fields
bent down to pluck an asphodel
it so aroused Pluto sexually he snatched her
and brought her down to the underworld
made her his wife
and muted his ears to her mother's piteous cries
—yet every spring for a fleeting glance you can see a lovely
flesh of Spring stoop to pluck an asphodel

"Not recognizing just the kind of person I was..."

Not recognizing just the kind of person I was
I continued what I thought to do was righteous

Little did I know how little I knew
I knew it was me in the mirror
I didn't see the slow change
Others saw, just as I saw the change in them

No wonder I didn't recognize me; the me's
And what I gave content to righteousness
was sheer dopiness

I thought acting like a fool
I'd make people happy and in turn they'd like me
Parentless, an orphan, horror about
I sure needed love—
I made sad people happy; I was liked
…but something was wrong

I was treated like a child—yet manhood confronted me
I got what I thought was love but it wasn't love
I felt like a jerk—

Yet the jerk was protected, like a mascot, nobody dare beat me
rape me, I brought joy to those sad men
commuted from death; serving life; fifty years;
I entered that prison the youngest and left the youngest
and I swear I saw tears in some eyes the day of my departure
Sad trouble was I came out as I left, a fool,
enough to make people laugh and hopefully like me

My manhood had been truncated, O damn'd life!

"I never really looked at my hands…"

I never really looked at my hands
As a teen I'd oft wish I had no hands
so that I'd never kill with them
I looked at them today—boy, are they old!

The knelt hands in prayer
The bowed hands in piety

Sportsmen used to slap each others asses
Now they high five each other
Is there a difference?
There is between the kiss and the handshake

Age, you can tell by the hands
Those face-lift jobs
they don't take away the brown spots
and thin wrinkles on the hands
…no hand-lifts, no magical creams

Old age? The hands are a dead give away

Mummified by time
…for men a strength is there
for women fragile as glass

"The illness of the winds…"

The illness of the winds
their contagion is legion
The blight of Dutch Elm disease
has not been contained in Buffalo—

It's all there
if only I can let it out all at once
I've got everything for you
all that a born poet is blessed to do
and, remember, it has to be in poetry
and all that poetry contains
like beauty, kindness, truth, compassion, etc.,
like things I hubrisianly threw away—
No, it takes work; older, it isn't so easy anymore;
indeed—what I was born for,
besides poetry
is death—
Like I feel it's a race.

"This is how it happened…"

This is how it happened:
At the end
everything that was
dwindled into a dot;
the dot exploded into the void
and the beginning began again—

As soon as he felt well enough
he rushed back
to where he loved to hunt mushrooms

The doctors prescribed complete rest
He prescribed himself complete silence
A soundless room his was
He even muffled his own sounds
walking on tip toe
holding in his gas

Music would not be music
were there no pause—

He put the nitro in a tea-spoon
put a candle-lit flame beneath it
and boiled it like he would dope…
he then dropped a small ball of cotton in the spoon
and drew out the substance with his spike…
done, he put his hypo in a case
and kept it close wherever he went—

He often kept it in the inside pocket of his jacket
One day a man who looked like Dr Mengele
came up to him and hugged him hard…
both were blown to smithereens—
Who was this man?

Jesus, da Vinci, Socrates…
who were these men?

The females:
A child-daughter; a lovely maiden in love;
a wife; a mother; a gold-medalist; a grandmother;
who is she?

The self and/or selves:
He speaking for myself
is somewhat akin to me;
I am of his kind;
but we are unalike;
nor am I like me all the time;
through bonding we understand each other
more than others;
that makes for friendship—

"I have a poem to tell…"

I have a poem to tell.
I couldn't tell it in prose or novel form…
Prose is writing in reality, but fictionalized reality. Now
poetry, poetry is dream; truthful; unveiled;
there need be no lengthy story (Fictionalizing;
fattening to the tale.) The poem is one word, or
an encyclopediac bushel of them.

Truth is the true reality; not the form; straight lines;
or the scrambled ones…with novel-writing you can
afford such play
      …imagination can incite, entice, all fakery;
it can give you unreal pleasures…

"I can predict with 99 percent accuracy…"

I can predict with 99 percent accuracy
the day after the event—
Once in a dream playing whist with FDR
"Tomorrow the Japs will do it, you know" I said
"Yes, I know" he replied
"That's it? I asked
"I sent out the aircraft carriers, did I not?
"Those poor guys on the battleships…"
"Churchill needs me…damn those isolationists!"
"Fuck the ships! can't we save our sailors?"
"It wouldn't smell right…besides the Japs will know
we broke their code"—

How to make propaganda out of theory?
Einstein was a master at it;
Yet Heisenberg is more my speed,
he, like Heraclitus, said it in words;
in fluidity: You can't step
in the same stream twice:—Once
you come upon the answer you lose it
because it changes before your eyes
by merely looking at it—

What am I doing?
I'm writing off the wall
I feel like I'm on a train
in Nazi Germany 1942
I'm afraid
Germans have faces like no one else
Hard, unsmiling, unless singing—
Maybe it's because I'm an orphan
I've no one anywhere—I wouldn't mind being lost in the
Schwarzwald like Hansel & Gretel, though—
O God help me—

And O how that sweet flowing liquefacation
of my time-melting face and hair falling away
leaving my swinging arms
creaky like marching wooden soldiers—

"Just look how Nestor-smashed the skin…"

Just look how Nestor-smashed the skin
crawling age becomes
…and this without anger or acid thrown

A fashion model was he not a pugilist;
he'd lotion his skin, shined his nails
…the whispers behind his back: Prune Face!

A loner, he'd mutter: There'll be payback time;
and he was dead serious; people are not to be messed with
…and the irony! he was polite, gentle, kind, a lover of life

It was funny the way the day came;
often as a youngster…especially seeing the old,
…I'd say to myself: I'm different than them

Yet I'd always feel: I'll be like them one day
—and when the day came it was like the day before
…overnight my hair turned white; teeth: gone
Young, you wait to get older, old you wait to die.

"There were two times…"

There were two times
If only I would have broken my back
The vertebrae
First when I was 24
I was riding on Duke Sedgwick's bike
A ten speeder; fell flat on my back
—nothing broke
Second time on a horse on Allen's farm
It sped fast; I fell
Lost of wind, I couldn't get up;
in time I did; again, nothing broken—

Everyone around the table
looked at one another
Something was wrong—
The flow and ebb of the accustomed motion
had ceased; there was a cranking sound;
something was terribly wrong,
something mortally wounded—

without a word
we all thought best to flee the table
…there was panic
the exit was piled with wriggling scratching screaming
        bodies

Thought
the greatest human force in the universe
Now coiled like a heap of erratic snakes
at a clogged exit
A pit of squirming thought
unable to slither exit free—

There's no equality between night and day
No duality betwixt sun and moon
Is the Tasmanian wolf akin to the Timber wolf? I'm not going
to lie to you, the coming years are going to be very tough

The saviors of the world are dying like flies
The best minds of his generation are dead

Don't tell me not to spell it out
Go to the mesa give a yell, a shout!
Five layers beneath the mesa are chunks of sea-shell
Hear the yea-sayers marking spots where dinosaurs fell
Soon Sinclair will mark the spot where black-gold shoots up

"Reader..."

Reader
were I to communicate with you
to dump my inner mess on you
then I would begin Dear Reader—

How I got to write to you
was when I got on stage
like an entertainer
I was a shy guy
Remember, I had to read to you
words wrenched from the very depths
of the soul
What pain!
A painter can paint pain
but he doesn't stand by his painting—
I soon realized drink or drug could see me thru
And that is the short and tall of it

YOU SAY BEAUTY, HOW FORTUNATE WE ARE: IT IS OLD OUR BEAUTY ALL OLD…DEATH FOLLOWS

True, you have della Francesca, we have de Kooning;
young we're young; I pray we grow beautifully old.
Crime has come down in NYC, yet they had to screw it up
and put Capital Punishment in it…no smart man, I don't care
how sharp a dude he be, no sharp man if he had chance to
scale weigh money or violence with a feather, feather always
ends up winner—
The condemned man pays his debt to society, me, you, the
sad uneducated fool didn't know that money don't mean
nothing, and lost temper an old old hurt finally risen to the surface—
No human of any god owes me such a debt.

It was just 6 years ago I spent two years here; the place
hasn't changed; Coppola was here gave me a part in
Godfather 3, his worst, remember, I played the unruly
stockholder, fittingly so—four days work, a thou a day, it was
great, chess with Pacino, he won;
was introduced to Al Martino as poet; I shook his hand, and
he said I don't like poetry. Eli Wallach was sweeter;
he said that whenever he heard poesy his toes twinkled.
I wish I could stay here, but you know? the place is the same
but the people are gone; and my best friend my poet friend
has died; I feel America needs me in a funny way.
Anyway I hope I yet divined with the gift—
I lose my inspiration
I lose my spirituality; and besides I don't feel sick; and
America doesn't seem sick, so who knows?! I got 3 years to
go to hit the year 2000—
I feel something wondrous is gonna happen
You know why? Because I've had a full life; screwed up a lot,
but getting right down to it, I have had one good trip.

"There is no time…"

There is no time
but spans and measures of the Eternal
Your time-piece as your finger prints
belongs only to you—

As the hunch you have is yours alone
so too your life-span measurable to none other—

And when long days and longer years
orbing sparks of void for us to make
our journey seaward with kept eye
on the celestial clock
…for what measured present ever now
will hold my face the true face;
no matter what mirror…
If there's no time how to stop it?
It must be something else that moves—
There's motion; there's orbing;
there's one step; there's two step…
Strange, if my face ages, why doesn't my mirror age?
I mean, both rhythmically at the same no-time?

"Used to be the stamps of Egypt…"

Used to be the stamps of Egypt
were frontal images of the Sphinx
the color of which was dirty crimson

All the other stamps of Egypt were of King Farouk
—all in varying colors
There were other stamps, of course
—but I'm dealing with the first pages of the album

There was Greece
A purple stamp
It depicted a ship
crossing the Corinth Canal
It was a plain stamp
—not as beautiful
as each wind rounding the Tower of Winds

The three stamps
of France's great poets:
Rimbaud, with the drunken boat;
Verlaine, seated in a bar
drinking absinthe;
Baudelaire, crawling
wisteria still as snakes

America, two stamps
I've always loved
One: The huge orange head
of Andrew Jackson
Two: The one dollar black stamp
of cattle in driven snow

Australia, I had its first stamp
a tan & white stamp of
a kangaroo

And New Zealand, a rare commemorative
of a famous falls in jungle green

The British Commonwealth: Large exquisite
colorful Mercurys leaning against globes
airmails good for every commonwealth country

Tannu Tuva: All triangle stamps
of musk oxen and huts of musk ox skin

The Penny Black of Queen Victoria
England's first stamp

The two inverted American stamps
One: a bi-plane
Two: a ship, or train?

Uganda's knuckle-posed gorilla

Lidice: silver-black SS profile of Heydrich

Poland Nazi Occupation: Large stamp of many shades
of brown of Adolph Hitler

Russia: Red-toned stamp of Lenin on stage fist raised

Japan: stamps depicting paintings Utamaro, Hiroshige, Hokusai

"Tell me not of time and places…"

Tell me not of time and places
of men who shaped the world
I've seen the spider at work
long after earth was twirled

How are you, you so beautiful
remiss of cancer; your cellophane skin
a see-thru like your eyes
whereby I see myself with weak smile—
How are you, did your hat get away from your head?
Were you dusted? No, not you, lipstick friend of Beauty—
Unmade-up your plainness was not Beauty in hiding…

I'll get back at them
with one master stroke:
I'll wait 3 weeks
then my vantage point
will be noisy front rooms;
it had to be carefully planned
All that was left to do was:—When

On your knees, get ready, set, crawl!
If you look hard enough you can
…spotting is an art
you're on the level of the roach;
long life to you—

"The dark underside of saintliness…"

The dark underside of saintliness
is plaster
Whether you proclaim to save the world
or take a vow of penury;
penalize those lower than yourself
and turning your head give a false smile—

Make not of solid dreams gooey,
the shadows of sleep are marrow'd bones
made in the image of their demons
like Chinese puppets behind a screen
opium realities with long noses and pointed hats

Flaubert in his robe and slippers in Cairo
writing to his mere when not to Salambo
For sure a person like me
could not live in his time
It was a time of unafraid men

Too late came the realization
that I was a no good bum
My only excuse was: Ignorance
is excusable when so;
inexcusable when not so—

Tell me something new
not that piece of veal I chewed
and put back on the plate
and you passing by picked it up
and chewed that leather I couldn't chew—
You are a very famous man and I shan't
reveal your name
simply because of a piece of chewed veal
It would embarrass you and what embarrasses another
embarrasses me double-fold

"The possibilities…"

The possibilities
they are many…
Life, unlike Time,
cannot be rewound;
what good possibilities galore
when the soft timepiece winds down?
Best venture a sparse impossibility—

Oh, the life line was thrown
I grabbed it with my dammed guilt
gave me a year ½ to breathe
It's an old tradition
having a patron;
the fair thing about mine,
he offered it; I asked not—
Now my angel my country atomized
is in that place where charity
is blood-sucked by reality
…the dreamer is being shook awake

He himself is an artist
He benefits me because he feels I'm deserved
Why I mention suffering guilt
is because I have yet to create
the creations he knows I'm capable of…
Patronage is age-old
as old as poetry
Tho it behooves one not to be at the behest of another
I know as my life line and health dwindle
I shall fold the whole scramble gently…neatly
Boy, what a piece of work am I—

Javert is closing in
I've yet to fulfill my task
The time is most inopportune
They're dying or dead my lifelong peers
All, all of them have succeeded;
have reached salvation

"Head—bowed like a bull…"

Head—bowed like a bull
breaching the blizzard
of Poe's cemetery
cursing "I don't care if I'll ever
look gigantically down…enough to have felt
what he felt"
Poetry is in the feeling of it
the feeling of creation is more than enough—

There was a closed bottle of cognac
on his snow-whipped grave
I saw the reflect of my face
as though my flesh by the sea—

I cried more for myself than for him
Poetry stands bright, flawless, eternal
when the poet of it is lain dead
but alive the poet stunts his spirit
becomes too human; older nearer the manticore—

I love the poets of the past;
I don't even really like the smell of the living—

"I wish I had a bear for a friend..."

I wish I had a bear for a friend
One I could cuddle up with come hibernation
Wash me with its tongue and dry me with its warm breath
Go by the upstream and slap the flip-flapping salmon
Eating all the eggless ones all day
Then lying on our backs rubbing our tummies
Gulping and belching with dopey smiles on our faces
O what wondrous warmy wonderfulness life can be!

The world shall partially end
as it last had 66,600,000 years ago
believed to have slammed into Mexico's
Yucatan Peninsula stirring up a cloud of dust
that blacked the sun's rays, created a nuclear
winter condition, and wiped out the dinosaurs
second, smaller asteroid hit the Pacific Ocean
off the coast of Chile 2 million years ago,
and, in 1908, a much smaller asteroid vaporized
six miles above the Earth in Siberia,
igniting fires and flattening trees
for 700 square miles

The Magic Fink
dressed in powder electric blue
though he was 33%
he was the Grand Canaria's shadow
And when his call went out
All Masons who were Masons came
These were the elite
They carried their leather cases with them
Rules, compasses, slide-rules, oval-pointed leads
attached to string, and plans—
The stone-cutters were the second elite;
proud to wear their compass conjoined rules
proud to wear their cultish ring of compass and rule

After the first millennium came to a close
the world thought the world was at an end
Now the second millennium is at hand
In two years the year 2000 will be upon us
The woodwork is creaking, viper-like tongues are flicking out
From out the far-away sky shall fall 20,000 mph
toward Earth wiping out all light and life
The true end shall come when the voice is silent
the word un-uttered, the churinga unstrung….
In the end the word will be mute; the song unsung;
no mouth to speak, no ear to hear, no eye to see—

"Do you know what they…"

Do you know what they
(that unnamable THEY)
want of me?
They want me to ignore the herms of Pan I pass;
desist from devotions when visiting Eleusis;
to cease acknowledging Demeter as my mother;
and, the absolute nerve, to stop using the raiment of Hermes
as petasus (the winged helmet); and caduceus
(the wand) and the loveliest of all talaria
(the winged sandals)—

No one's fault but mine own
It used to be I wrote for my learning;
the "generation" thing got into it
and it was the public I was teaching
…destined was I for a terrible hubrisian fall—

IN THE END WAS THE WORD

In the middle 1950s
toward the end of the 2nd year of 1960
I'd five books of poetry in print—

The decade of the 1970 saw one book;
1980 saw another—

'Tis the middle of this decade: 1990
Another decade's work—
The task is typing it up.
The poems will consist of the '80s & '90s—
Now if my wish sees it through with me
and I live to the year 2000
—I feel I can rightfully exclaim:

A work begun hath become a work done—
Behold! that I began in the mid '50s
and close in the mid '90s
…publishing, that is
I wrote my first poem 13—silly poem:
"Three flowers without a stem
three for a nickel, who wants them?"
Silly, yes—but where did that feeling
for the slaughter of flowers come from?
O I did unkind too—
A duad was I! Born of cave people, ignoranti, testa duras!
With the divineness of spirits spun into my capote of fleshedness
There's a reason dopey wisdom and me; a reason poetry and me;
a reason lovelessness and me; a reason the hubris of knowledge
is no longer my master; a reason I embrace faith unto me—

2.

The word not spoken
is not in that Miltonic guy's head of definitions,

he sitting lowly and bowed
at the edge of the firmament—
Wasn't in Prometheus' pig-skin of gifts:
The demigods of eons past felt a care for people;
The Giver of Humankind alone giveth!
Terrible his eternal punishment
offering humanity what was his not to give: Fire

The snake was what his form and name deemed him:
The Tree of Life damned humanity to ignorance forever
(And I used to claim I'd rather a bit of knowledge
than a whole lot of faith) There's hubris for you—
Faith bring forth intelligence, not intelligence, Faith—
Whether it be hubris or no—of late I've been saying:
I feel more for humankind than I do Life—
Life it is hurts humankind: suffering, illness, unkindness—

3.

What's a full day?
Where rose the sun this morn
is where I watched it rise yestermorn—
My watch at first sight of the sun was 6:15;
when I saw the same tip of the sun rising
my watch had 6:15 ½ —

To the American Indian a full day and the exact land for living
was the time it took to walk from dawn to dawn—

Like all clocks, those two are multiple variables;
Time does not exist…'tis a dimension of man—
Now regard how long dinosaurs have been dead?
Okay, regard how long the child born 3 days from now,
regard how long the eons it took for it finally to become!
Hark this, space is not affordable, room for only one—

Time, great inflation of it; think how silly:
They sentence a guy to die for a crime;
to him time becomes precious
[...]

4.

In the mental cosmos
as is without…the megagalaxy
I with all humankind am cosmic megamind

The Space Traveler runs on fraudulent time
whereas the poet travels in Word Past
Therein the Word never spoken resides
When discovered in its written form
It will be humankind, the understander of the poet,
shall stentor the Word spacequaking the cosmos
which is finite; and spare the Absolute, which is Infinite
—all that is is finite; all that isn't infinite—

Space exists—time is non-existent
O SpaceTime continuum!
Pray tell, if the epitome of Space is Infinity
how then, if there's no time
…what's the epitome Eternity thrones?

I beg that Faith enlighten me and thus you;
I have no doubt it will appear in this book—
The Word exists because it is part of the finite;
the words that exist are minor, those that don't are
    absolute—

what if that Unspoken Word of yours
doesn't exist—what if it's non-existent; a nothing
of the Absolute—

What's wrong with an endless finite, man-created time?
Life's okay—in the end is the word—
I don't care how in tune you are with your spirit, muse,
whatever you call them: No word shall transplant the tree;
And what about these things called MYTHS;
they're dead, correct? They were Gods once, correct?
Like marble. All I wish to know is who marbled them dead?
Again I say it's the fault of TIME—
The Christian God of today could never be as cruel
to leave Prometheus atop that rock, vultures eating his bones
—for Eternity! See! There is no time ergo no eternity!
The snake conned them into being clones of their master;
instead he cloned them into him, that poor lonely...
that I have no faith in time then: in the beginning;
in the end—beginning; end—Prometheus Unbound, Shelley knew!
The Son of God, did He not promise to return?
I can only guess, He could restore Eden; He could forgive Lucifer
He could empower Life to end human suffering to...enough
I pray for that cathartic day of FAITH
when gone my immature smile and the silence of my spirit
in stentor roars into my ear the Word I wrote unknowingly—

5.

There's an order to things
Nature's familiar flukes
contains nothing doomsday
Human order needs law to enforce
A typhoon kills thousands
A beserk kills all the McDonalds customers

a man dies in his late 60s;
a guy says: "He lived a full life, nice job, wife—
Full life? It was only yesterday I was in my 50s!

How brave those guys landing at Normandy!
I guess confronted with it, the fear goes
What's there to fear—life's heavy shit;

So you die, big deal; you have no idea you're dead,
all you simply did was bum out friends, if you had any—
But I tell you, there's something to say about youth—
Death doesn't exist in the dictionary of youth—
The man was on the money: It's a pity youth is wasted on the young
Said the other sage: Never enter a hospital voluntarily—
Imagine watching I Love Lucy in hospital bed 89 years old

It's only when you age you think this way;
when young nobody ever died; now old, I hardly know
    anybody
—young your youth was still ahead of you;
now in your years the days get older; but for your genes
you'd be dead by now—
I heard it blew your mind when you realized your cat
will outlive you—
In the past, say the 70s, I'd write 10 years work in 2 weeks
Two weeks is history—I call upon my spirit now,
my new gained Faith—
4 years never meant a clock existed for me—
Why 4 years? I like the coming of the millennium,
as well as coming century, and closing decade—

The mental constellation is etched in my brain;
all my papers of words was writ when I shot a word like a star
on the page…I claim no order, only a mystery,
one the sole duty of vates, to benefit Spirit/Life—

Rid of time—what was said year 1; is said now—

6.

A new dawn…never do I remain unwell for long;
As anger, never am I angry for long
My Doctor came to me in my sleep
Without Faith Charlemagne never would have been
He told the head tree-worshiper:

I WORSHIP HE WHO MADE THE TREE
And thus converted the Saxon Druidians—
Faith brings knowledge, not knowledge Faith!
The years it took to realize such simplicity
…hubris, it was: it sounded smart:
I'D RATHER A LITTLE BIT OF KNOWING THAN A
LOT OF FAITH
No wonder I'd tell certain people I'm not done yet
My work is incomplete—No, those early poems are great
they'd say—I knew better; only I could sense the emptiness
gnawing at my spirit. What insight had he, true "imaginary poet"
I never finished grammar school
Why Poetry? Why to me?
I had nobody, all I had was myself,
expressing words, ideas and forms, to myself
I had a friend: Me—
and poetry was great for someone not knowing much to say
I swear it was like a magic
The feeling I'd get when I saw that in 4 lines I had a poem
I was given the chance to write in notebooks because
I entered prison at 16 1/2 and left December 1949
During those years I ate up the prison library,
the Standard dictionary of 1905
—that's how I learned all the archaic & obsolete words—
Went through Bulfinch Mythology;
I didn't know they had the best Oxford dictionary there—
—later I was told it was the best encyclopedia ever, 1911
So it could be said I went to the school of hard knocks—

This work is to be read, studied, at many sittings;
deem it hubris on my part, but this is the work that saves me;
my second chance shall knight my salvation
with the seven angels of the Muse—
13 years after birth I deemed myself POET
As my oldest friend and Wordsworth to Coleridge
once dedicated to TO A PURE IMAGINARY POET

I ask the best poet of my time; whatever fated us
meet 46 years ago—we met with poetry unknown us,
two strangers we talk the talk I love: beauty
and the shocker we both believed without a doubt
we were bonifide poets—A street kid; and ward of the state,
I had no idea what poetry was; what poetry meant?
I wrote a silly poem at 13, at 15 I wrote what I felt powerful
A few weeks before my 17th year I heard in my cell voices
which I wrote down; wasn't long before I received a book
called Ideas & Forms in English & American Lit.—
First came Beowulf; the Twa Sisters; Sir Gawain and the
Green Knight—they did nothing for me; it was when Smart;
Herrick; Hood; Marvel; Milton; and the immortal Romantics,
I came upon the other half of the duad: Poetry.
I wasn't born poet; no one told me there existed such as:
Poetry. I never graduated from grammar school.
It came to me, poetry. I was a boy who lived alone.
Poetry became my friend. It was possible to confide in it.
I had something to talk to; and something that talked to me.
I never asked a soul to read a poem of mine—
I cared not whether they liked it or no;
I knew who I was; I had been visited upon by poetry.
My earliest delve into hubris was my believing there was no
better poet amongst the living than myself—
I oft asked myself why I did not ask the poets I met:
"I say, can you be so kind as to inform me how poetry
came to you? When, how, did the word come to you?
Your first poem, did you know it to be such?
Is it not true that any given age more than one poet
I mean great ones, exist?"

It was hard for me to believe a person
any person
especially those I knew
would end a life, theirs, as immortal as Burns, Lovelace—
Statues of them; stamps of them; streets named after them!

The famed dead had my complete devotion,
whereas the supposedly famous living
their presence brought queeky voices; they'd belch!
I hated their egos, the smell of their flesh;
I'd rather adore a dead lousy poet than a good living one
A verse is a poem of one line
or a verse can contain 20 or more lines to make a poem
The cloaked Poe lived by night crossed a bridge
and looked at his face gigantically down in the sea below—
His day lacked electricity yet he held an agate lamp in hand.
Poets should live as phantoms, reclusive like Emily D.

"She poemed her words in circles…"

She poemed her words in circles
I saw it on a lined page
written on both sides
before the owner, dying of cancer,
sold it for 8,000 dollars
to a London collector—

to finger the dewy warmth of morn
wisteria between the fingers
with eyes upon the slow motion of stems climbing
toward a magnetized sunlight
until the burst of flowered colors

to be is space
not to be is time
eventually
space is to be replaced
time is not to be eternal

the spirit of command
had experienced a mix-up
Nothing planned from childhood to manhood
anticipated the mental-physical snafu
Paranoia set in; perhaps the fault was hubrisian
or the wrench of olding screwed the works
For sure it convinced him that poetry was sacred;
that the miracle was not for the wanting;
poetry is no thing unilateral
—something beside the poet is enjoined

Decade—Century—Millennium

1000—2000; 1900—2000; 1990—2000
To these three changes of time
I in my 70th year shall give testimony—

"Make some friends…"

Make some friends
A good friend, now dead
said "Once they know you
"you'll never make friends again"

Women are different; they're more than a friend
But I don't chase them anymore
My hair, like I foretold,
turned white overnight;
In Paris 1967 I went to a bistro
I felt my pockets, I left my money home
Thank Hermes I didn't eat
I got up and hurried out
the maître d' followed me out
punched my mouth
not one word passed between us
he loosened my teeth
about six months later my gums stank
I suffered every tooth its insufferable ache
To rid myself of gum-stench and toothache
I had them all pulled out
I bled for five days
At 37 I was toothless
The toothless lion waved goodbye to poetry readings
couldn't get the "f's" out
but I owed a debt to hubris and arrogance
so drink was all it took
to get me back on stage and play out
that Blue Angel chicken guy—

But that was 30 years ago
and during those years
regardless the losses
I loved four women
stayed five years with each
and gave each a cameo of me

All are happy
I always keep friends with women
It was age stopped the chase
Though some did come to me
Losses of youth are losses of vanity
Age with the losses is another thing
Face your Fate in olding with a smile
like a wrinkled Eskimo—

"In the first edition…"

In the first edition
he had two eyes
In the late edition
it seems one fell out of its socket
Was times like that caused me befuddlement—
The Lone Ranger was a pip!
I must have been 11 or so and saw in the papers
that he had been killed in a head on car crash
yet that very night as was our custom
we tuned in the Lone Ranger and there he was with his:
Hi-ho Silver, away!

A perverse hubris seemed to tally
nothing I targeted…there are only two ladders to climb
and oddly enough I climbed down
without climbing up…go figure

Bad guys, their name is legion;
I only wished I climbed up the first ladder
then coming down the second would have made sense

"Dear Saintly Dr Luke…"

Dear Saintly Dr Luke:

You beloved of the Son of God; He of compassion
and all-knowing; they who ate of the Tree of Ignorance;
have emblazoned your divine name on a hospital whose
bottom line is money; whose stay at the methadone ward
costs 1000 dollars a day, whose food is equal to a soup
kitchen's; who have orderlies serve as bona-fide nurses; their
task is to take your blood pressure & temperature anytime
they catch you stroll the main hall; they serve the juices and
constant sandwiches where the word redundancy was never
given thought—what cared the patients, Medicaid held
them beholdant to the state—

What cared Mr Smithers? My money and the welfare
unfortunate were equally bankable—From there I went to
the take-out clinic. I received the same medicine, only this
time, it cost me 60 dollars a week; I saved over 7000 dollars a
week—A drug taker is a sick person, yet they were treated
like the Nazis treated the Jews; the contempt and
mightier than thou dispensers of a drug just as addictable
as heroin, these dealers (no different than those of the
street) except the non-nurses showed more understanding,
of course it can be said of all bureaucrats, they are of many
not of one; all automatons, of one mind, such as holds
proximity to tyranny—

I feel compassion for your kind; you labor there all day;
I visit in the minutes. The sad ignorance is you hate so your
work, those who make your work possible, the victims of the
pain of life; are treated not as patients but as the fallen by
self choice; you made thy bed now sleep in it—Such is not
the philosophy a Hippocrates extend future humankind
I desire not Medicaid; I earn a living by giving lectures
such as to school kids: Mother Earth made the rose as she

made the poppy, tis all a matter of choice; my choice was to kill the pain of life…so I chose the filthy nurse, heroin.
To pay for what others get free; I needs work; Never was I given a take out—my urine was dirty; I got a letter from my doctor explaining why I had taken what I had;
I owe no one lie; a few drinks were never a constant; heroin perhaps no more than 3 times a whole year, why? no take out—Coke is not my drug; what else? If I were dirty why come in? One may understand, but a mob, no—
Granted druggies can find many excuses; but a father who orphaned me off; who whipped and gave me up to orphancy, is soon to die;

I want to make it clear before the time spent on this earth—I had no idea he had Alzheimer's; haven't seen him over 10 years, he's 86; he lives in San Antonio Texas—he and my younger brother came visit me—He could not be left alone; my brother cared for him; it was awful; I helped wiped the ass of the monster who almost killed my 16 year old mother; she fled, left him, and me forever——I didn't want his death, unfulfilled in life, on my consciousness!

"Reader, when poetry came to me…"

Reader, when poetry came to me
I never meant it for you

I was an orphan
she mothered me, the Muse

I was a ward of the Church
I was doled out to loveless
needy families; 6 of them;
each one had a single dark room for me
My only companion was my imagination
I did not know then
but now I know
I was born of the Muse
…that's why in life I was mean to poets
I claimed Her for my own
The only poets I ever liked were the young dead ones

It never made a difference to me
if mine was a hubrisian claim
Full well I know
to have experienced the birth of the poem
Undeniable, O God, undeniable the feeling of it
Faith, I adore you your salvation—

Was the time of world depression
I was born into it an orphan
a ward of the Catholic Church
From birth to my 10th year
I was doled out two years or less
to 6 needy loveless strange families—
A man visited me once a year
He sat upright, hard looking,
talking with my foster parents
…hardly did he look at me;

after coffee they said their goodbyes;
before he left, he entered my room with me
…closed the door behind him and wham, wham,
two stinging slaps to my face.
"Behave" he ordered, and left.
Was years later I learned he was my father.
He punished me for having spilt Jello
on myself, hot yet! 8 months ago,
a thing I was already punished for!
I hated leaving my room.
And feared the day when the yearly visitor visited—

"When the one of the many that came…"

When the one of the many that came
and spoke well of new things
ears were alerted but eyes slowly scanned the field
and mouths tightened—
Swamis had peacocks do their bidding
Orators foretold of unseasonal weather
Astrologers contradicted each others' omens
Then like a flash!
Four men were stripping a BMW in a Bronx garage
"Where you sending Pancho?" asked one of the four.
"To diplomatic school, Carrol, I think, it's near Tufts
"I want him to be a Presidente one day"
"First he's got to learn Mexican, no?"
"This America, here he can learn anything"
FLASH!
The Emperor declaimed: "All astrologers leave Rome!"

Saul had a flash and became Paul
When there's a bad smell you run away from it
Dumbstruck, frozen like in a dream, no fumigations to
    release
from the silos
the dead sackcloth girl is skeletal now beneath the corn

"I don't know how you could have been a different me…"

I don't know how you could have been a different me
The night before happily tipsy in a London bar
something I said upset the painter Lucian Freud
at the table was my favorite painter Bacon
I don't recall what I said;
anyway the next morn I came upon Mr Freud, smiled and waved;
he blurts out: "That's all right, you weren't yourself"
Walking away I was confounded; a Freud telling me
I wasn't myself?
"Then who the heck WAS I?"

Actually I have three favorite living painters: Francis Bacon
—Balthus—and de Kooning—

Who was I, indeed.
If Freud doesn't know;
then surely the only one who knows is Gregory, by me!

I know I'm more than one
but my behavior when having drunk
where I'm unable to hold my mud
I don't count that a different me
just a not in control me…still me—
I rarely hear of a murderer let off for having been drunk;
insanity is an excuse, drunkenness not—
Yet how many sad souls wake up the next day and
scream in horror "O God! what have I done?"
Mean temper, no good…poor humanity—

"The captain just went down…"

The captain just went down
the first mate years ago
the radioman a few weeks before the captain
The cook got the best obit of all
the ship is sinking fast
The cabin boy joined the crew

gathered in the late 40's
in the early fifties or end of the 40's
He was part of the crew when the ship left port and
delivered their cargo—
The radio man kept it all together
I graduated and another cabin boy took my place
He was the radio man's constant mate—
We two are all that is left
and the ship is sinking—

My cargo is unfinished
I hope to deliver it before she goes down
if not
I pray I go down—unfinished
the gift unfulfilled

Who claims I was hubrisian?

"Beauty falls lithely down…"

Beauty falls lithely down the number one reason
the stairwell was built as was the fountain
in the center of the grand ballroom

Driblets like pearls water falls the crystal
piddling rings to the edge of the pool
an endless widening of perpetuation
—O let's dive into that print
　　　of eterne motion
and not testify to the skin-covered ill

I couldn't tell if there was concern on their faces
Perhaps it was because I was joking
like: I'm too old to die—

I can't stand the white color smell
of hospitals and swimming pools

I'm 69 and I have no SS, Medicaid, Medicare
What about the biop, the Big C, who'll pay?
I'll bargain a souk of docs with poems—

I once asked an Athenian: When
does a boy for men
become a man for boys?

Mid-life crisis is more insufferable
than old age waiting to die
Old:—There's no fear of dying

The milky pink
and diamond blue
Of Albion's flesh and eyes

"Be constant in your righteousness…"

Be constant in your righteousness
each right benefiting the coming right
like Ford Model T's rolling full
and perfecto off the assembly line

It's so sad to see failure in the eyes of others
People know
How?
Because you know—

Truth you need not remember
But your lies are insufferably unforgettable

What good the truth though
…nobody ever took me on vacation
At least I got a box of turkish delights for lying

If you live a righteous life though
the reward is awesome
All your years to come
will contain the most heavenly memories
like an engagement with it on earth
and a marriage to it in heaven—
Yes, it pays to be good and beautiful in life

Yes…yes

"And who may I ask are you?…"

"And who may I ask are you?"
"Me"
"Does 'Me' have a name?"
"Yes, You"
"Me? Gregory?"
"Gregory, yes, or Nunzio"
"We're one and the same, I take it"
"Yup"
"Talking to myself again"
"What else is poetry but talking to oneself?"

"I thought poetry was the poet in communion with God"

Nothing will pre-empt the coming Tuesday
with next week caught in a deadly swirl
of cat and mouse later this month;
Wednesday's schedule has been adjusted—

Your Kalend is equipped with a device
that allows the Thursday to skip
if, that is, you do not wish to wake that day—

Yes, I know what you're thinking;
there is a conspiracy afoot
…but the first 3 days of December
corresponds to the appropriate numbers
pursuant to the Mayan Vatican codices—

Remember
Remember how important and great a find
the Apollo Belvedere
It's in some corner of the Vatican Museum now,
nigh forgotten—

I was there when Pius died
he was lain oblong on a slab
they were singing Mozart's Requiem;
all about Roman town young men
flowed in long red and black gown—

"The 3 of Ice…"

The 3 of Ice
has sinned upon the sparse Earth
by the deviser of Time

And by whose glaciations did fatten the seas

the primal human family walked out of Africa

Did they ship across the seas as well?

There wasn't a port that a rat
never skittered down the rope
Upon departure no port lacked the sight
of a long pale arm lain across it

Dip a red hot iron into a pewter mug of beer
and catch between the sizzle and whisperings
word of sails from the east seen from the Widows Walk

Ice man time 3 degrees
The steaming snout of the Wurm's wooly mammoth
twirled thru the snow…mountains took shape

Who secretly turns against his master
will ever carry the stain of slave
Overthrow or slay openly
elsewise suffer the fate of Enkidu
when he silently opened the gate
to slay the monster orphan
rather than kick in the gate and dispatch him thus

"Would you have me believe he walks with spiked feet…"

Would you have me believe he walks with spiked feet;
Heads towards my kind with open giving hands
blood crusted with the skin of nails?

The nights were Spring nights or Autumnal nights
those wondrous nights in Greenwich Village—
The people all young, villagers and tourists alike;
the artists, poets, dancers, actors, Bohemians all—
They were on the move in the 20's, 30's, 40's
but after the war, all stayed, apartments were cheap;
boys and girls lived together, gays lived without hassle,
poems and paintings all day, bars and wine all night—

This time of time
the lives of our time
are falling like fireflies
'Tis the touch of the icy hand with warmth
hath come to leave me sans fireplace
and in solitaire—
Alone I be in a life once filled with angelic spirit—
Faith comes before intelligence
Faith is strengthened by knowledge
I used to claim: I'd rather a mite of knowledge
than a barrelful of faith—
How lost was I!
O Origen, Augustine, Clement, how true!
One needs faith to gain knowledge;
there is no knowledge got
by lack of faith—
Knowledge is what we know;
faith is what we do not know—

What we know is finite
What we don't know infinite

Who are these people that were Aztec?
The heart, their most precious possession,
fed to the sun to keep it on the run—

"They know your condition…"

They know your condition
The dispenser gives you the antidote
They all watch you
Your anxiety is plain
You must wait
They're all familiar with your condition
"It'll soon kick in," you're assured
I'm amongst losers
It was all right when I was young
But an olding loser…Hope is short of time

The wings of the bee
buzzes a trail of *zzzzzzzs*
as it sways thru the redolent breeze
in the busy pheromonian night

"If things of no import…"

If things of no import
disturb the balance of things,
disturbances occur
and become important—

It's not DON'T MAKE WAVES
it's keeping the imbalances in check
OVERFLOW is the big no-no
Such things are the sheep
and we're the shepherds accountable
…to the point: O.K., to bottom out on the balances;
the scale never changes
—only randomly does a weight unintentionally (?)
drop on the plate

It's the way such things are done
Tipping the scales
is the same as skimming from the top—
It can go on indefinitely
unless greed
the weights fall more frequently
then alas the disturbances
the unaware become aware
the alarm rings OVERFLOW—

Caught
it's all finished
There are no excuses
I'm a social wreck is no excuse

To Faith
which came late to me
Boy, hubris is hell to pay
But to balance the scale
with heart and feather
No excuse
I always knew better—

"Old age wills but once…"

Old age wills but once
whether to live or die is not of choice
Chance either random or select
shall mark the spinet's turn and raven's dive

Change alone shall sand the hour's flow
The timing destined and just
Again the birth shall come with ignorance
O no one mother, one father!

Born of oneself like asparagus
Ever rooted embilic'd to earthdawn
All the same-lived Days of Life
Allotted the Human Span
Great Year after Great Year
From Aries to Pisces
Round and round the Zodiacal Wheel
Each spoke 2000 years
12 spokes a full turn 24000 years
24000 did earth's span 167000 times turn
The multiplication of which deems earth's age
4,000,000,000

The depths vibrate the deep

as pheromones on the surface
trill the night air

The time is always near
to betray one's dreams
stab oneself in the back—
As one fated to greet one's mother
67 years after birth—

MY KARMA RAN OVER MY DOGMA

Did I write this? Say it?
I don't recall reading it,
or having heard it…
It's my kind of humor
i.e., witty iconoclastic;
yet it's something like
only Anon can give signature to—
Still, it's not that common
that it can be deemed cliché;
obvious truths, nameless, often become clichés

Sometimes a witty remark
is actually a thing of sarcasm
Sometimes telling the truth
is downright snitching

What is beauty, my beauty,
when in your eyes my eyes
like crystal balls for me to scry
and mine for you to scry
…do you love what you see?
Do I, scrying yours?
We see ourselves in each others eyes;
we do not reflect one another—
I gaze at the beauteous oak
I need not faith to believe
my eyes reflect it—
The clear still pool mirrors me
kneel beside me and look into my eyes

"And when all was said…"

And when all was said
and hardly heard
—the lasting man carried the weight
of the last words said

Deep from the freezing heart it came
(the least caring could only feel pity)
Life, it was supposed, was like that;
like so much happens and matters not…

If chance were given, O ye of little faith,
the odds would have it
you'd trouble yourself to understand why
the words of a man so sadly contrite
confronted ears so ridden with snowy silence—

For life of solid yet so soft white
it would be just as it was
for the man-made man whose end was so;
desolate, cold, humanless…

and still
even were those words heard
there was nothing of substance said
nor could be added: The pity of it—

Then if appeals can work
I appeal to those innocents never heard
and moreso those who ne'er spoke
This world as you see it
is not seen likewise by me
nor your gods
e'er match mine—

"Don't tell me crocodilians head for the hills…"

Don't tell me crocodilians head for the hills
Wooly mammoths would trudge the Alpine heights

on the wayside belly up
an ibis lay
Flat against the reeds
the howler monkey
is in sun-dried clay
the caiman smooths along the Nile

I never met anyone like me
Certain traits I found an affinity with
But it made me uncomfortable
They were creepy traits in others
"But surely I'm a pain" I assured myself

There's no less abolished
than the man tied to a pole
with a FIRE in unison
and his head drops above the ground
never to land
Though dead
the coup de grace to the head
is, though useless, an extra abolishment—

And the ball is head-bound
into the net's gape
The roar is a one-sided sound
Fists fly and the game takes shape—

where are the protective arms of love
used to shield me from the elements
my self-destructiveness
and that caring right arm swung across my chest
when she pressed the brakes?

Never knowing a mother's kiss
nor cradling arms
I was a deformity of love

evil, like a pack of afric dogs
know to circle the infant of the panicky horde

"Soul sickness devils the brain…"

Soul sickness devils the brain
Bereft of Faith spores the mind
The heart trembles in fear of God-Ignorance
The weak bodies of the irreligious
lack the gracelight of immunity—

Health with God is health in God
The Godless live less than the believers
Those who walk with God survive life's sojourn

When the faithful gather inside and warm
and the storm without is harsh and nary a soul
trees cringe beneath the electricities
and the pheromones of the ephemera hum the distances

When the after rains of a day
leave the redolence of magnolia in the Southern air

And when finally it comes down to the real
play it as always Leave me alone, I'm dreaming

Trouble is, they catch you in the end
Even if it takes 400 years like the Count St Germain
who was seen on earth twice
400 years apart—

Nothing to do with reincarnation
It works simply: Replacement & Return;
that is: Spirit leaves body;
Spirit returns in new body
born of new blood, new mind—
The one exception, the one similarity:
Spirit:—Eternal and Absolute—

"Deep—deep—deep within…"

Deep—deep—deep within
so deep I am ever unable to reach bottom
Once I ventured the deepest ever;
when I panicked I was stuck like a diver
not knowing up from down
I was going down
and broke through—

Life from then on
was painful to urinate
—whenever I had it burned
Then my right side at the waist
where the liver was throbbed
a soft pain—

Now I know
I never did come up
It's down I go
Round and round I go

You know I always believed in Godness
It's just that I didn't want people to know
It was something I had to work out
My belief was in a good God
One who knew and cared about me
I couldn't let anyone know
about my special God
My confused relationship with Him

Nothing ever happened bad to me
when I was raised Catholic

except for the Catholic foster-parents
6 in all
they just adopted me so they could get money from the Church

They didn't love me
They were stuck in the Depression
Anyway I never connected Godness with the actions
of people
That picture in the Foundling Hospital
I was the curly black-haired kid
sitting on Jesus' knee—

"Who taught me the song I sang?"

Who taught me the song I sang?
More a lament… and such cannot be taught—
Have I failed to show proper concern
for the afflicted heart?
Arrows, all arrows think you my words
shot from some insincere bow?
My lyres are clean; none are of dark stain—

No man is measured by how much he loves
but by how much he's loved—
If the heart be truthful the lyre
will of light always be—
I learned the song I taught
with goodness the intent of my reward—
That my song were a lamentation
examples no reward were due
—the love given is the love received;
as the song sung is the song heard.

"I despise the intrusive telephone..."

I despise the intrusive telephone
When it rings I immediately say I'M WORKING
before I ask who it is—
It's a good put off;
who dare interrupt a poet at work?
IT'S ME YOUR SON, NILE—
Oh that's another can of fruit salad;
How are you, I love you etc etc etc—

Riiiing! I'M WORKING
Wait, you promised you'd read tonight!
I quit reading; I can't face people;
believe it or not, I'm shy;
I have to get drunk to read
and never the serious ones do I read
I read the funny ones, to make people happy;
to make them like me…it's pathetic!
How can I give out the depth of my soul
to strangers! People should read the dead poets—
I'm an embarrassment when I read;
Keats will never embarrass poetry—
Also not only have I quit reading publicly
…I've become a recluse—
All I'll do for the rest of my days is
write poems, and hopefully have them published—
Riiiing! Why pick up the phone, let it ring—
No…it'd drive me nuts; why not disconnect? Yes.

"Space is in motion…"

Space is in motion
but time has no wheels—

Stars know no illness
they orb & spiral in rotation
yet die they do
and black holes have tombstones their seals

Galactic rings like diamonds on black velvet
halo my spaciousness
I face the universe alone like all of us—
How worthy we are to be regaled in all this absolute
Where was I
before the day 1?

On a tripod in the Gobi
in a suitcase on the first street corner

Who sold me?
Who bought me?

He with two hands on one arm;
buy, sell, buy, sell, back and forth
from hand to hand
…endlessly buying and selling me to himself—

To be rid myself of this insufferable redundancy
I chopped off his buying hand
and with the intact other I was sold
along with all the other goodies in the suitcase
the stars, moon, sun, the entire megagalactic wonder
…as for who bought me, I entered life an orphan—

The mother of Russia loved her children
yet the mother of the Russian child loved only hers

"He was five kilometers…"

He was five kilometers
from five kilos of…

Old whiskered ill Verlaine
was in the Sante awaiting death
He wrote his autobio there
only mentioned how much he loved
toy soldiers, not a word
about Rimbaud…

When I'm old enough
I'll become fast-acting
Walk with my arm around Ramses 2
talk to him like a buddy
and in my old charming manner
ask him for some gold…

Truth is unforgettable
Lies are forgettable
Truth never gets caught
Caught in a lie is a cliché
A cliché is repetitive truth

And if he walk away from the threat
of a gang of his peers
with the electricity of violence
crackling the hateful air
I'd have a jump in time
return to the Years of Past
and intrude a giant bear into the gang
with paws swinging away
and the threatend one stop
and hold his ground—

I have good reason to believe
there are hidden poisons amongst us—

Any frightening mix from elements in nature
unseen, odorless, can be mason jarred
on any shelf in any cellar in America—

Asked: And why were you there that day?
He answered: I was just there
He left and no one ever saw him again—

The others, they all knew why they were there;
It was a day all anticipated
…except for the guy that was just there

"The drums are beating…"

The drums are beating
somebody in hut 8 is cheating
O yeah, O yeah, the goats are bleating
somebody in hut 8 is cheating

"Before Time began…"

Before Time began
there was Eternity;
before the Finite
there was Infinity;
when the egg of Eternity
enjoined with the sperm of Infinity
…thus the birth of Time and Space
With the end of the Steady State
(the Mind cannot conceive the age
    of the Steady State)
came the Big Bang (the mind can surmise
    the age of the Big Bang: 14 billion years)

It takes a Mind to conceive the Big Bang
It takes No-Mind to example the Steady State

Without Mind
no thought to think
Without mind
no imagination to create
Without mind
no idea to conceive
Without mind
no conception of Godness
Without mind
nothing ever was

Before mind
there was eternity
Before mind
there was infinity
Both eterne and infinite
lay in steady state
wed in Absolute Void

The sperm of Eternity
entered the egg of Infinity
The Space-Time continuum was born
In time the mind was born
and as it evolves
it makes time a measurement of eternity
and space various distances of the finite

The Big Bang was the birth of God

"deviled-eye..."

deviled-eye
piercing my side
twisting rib of adam
man
showing itself to be a horror
of glazed spirit
in purest sullied form
overlarge orb
yellowed about the pupil
blinking rhythmic devil swell
spitefully rifle-eyeing
mewing beasts w/ souls

4/5/98

"the need is there..."

the need is there
humming
in my lungs & aching ears
buzzing congestion smoking through
leftover nights
typing one-handed
w/ scented fingers
nicotine whiff
tobacco scorched hours
lengthening
reaching out more & more real
nasty quiet walls
plugging away
at a plaster hoax—
if this building burns
while i'm bumping my head
in some inconvenient dream
puzzled at the shocking relevance
of a patchwork quilt
& i'm smoldering toes first
nestled soul not taking any notice
what will these walls be then
other than burning & blackened
from indelible smoke prints
well, no more a barrier
than they are right now
blasting their leper scalp residue
as usual, see
when the golden bowl is busted
and i seep out airy & silent
singing celestial monotone
the pillared salt mines won't matter
anymore
neither will the silken eyes & glassy hair
backwards & untouchable like porcelain dolls

not more animate than i was in life
only more difficult to throw stones at
& somehow clear as to direction
as i ascend automatic
pillaged realms
pristine dreams
to be part of god.

4/19/98

the muse

at the moment before I acknowledge it
i arrive in between
nothing
and entirely inside
cemetery-like and stoned
epitaphs sprouting from my eyes
nickels on my tongue
I prophecy naught but the senses relinquish
spasmic with spiritual restraint
—let go
(but they prod spidery with invisible shadowy webs)
"is this a dagger I see before me"
mystic with steel in sabbath dark
cock crow in the courtyard blood
robed in high-sentence
she glides inside
a bitter chalice boiling butter and honey
her dugs sexless
her sex forlorn
jingling trinkets from crown to crown
picking up prostrate boys ambition
tonguing ears with spirit

3/27/98

"My ancestral home was the cave…"

My ancestral home was the cave
A recurring dream would come to me
when awake & when asleep
—Myself and a pylon of wooly mammoths
trudging up a snowy alpine;
downward a Neanderthaler plain…

I would be frost bitten
with puffed belly starved
trudging the windy snows
looking homeward in circles
encircled by mountains
no stepward path to climb
but ever upward
and deep within wishing to fall where I hardly stand
and sleep my life away—

INDEX OF TITLES AND FIRST LINES

AAAAA — on the page	*41*
Ah, Micheline	*91*
A man gets older	*66*
And because the cause of it	*31*
And when last told	*62*
And when all was said	*153*
"And who may I ask are you?"	*144*
Ask me not of moons	*50*
at the moment before I acknowledge it	*170*
Beauty falls lithely down the number one reason	*142*
Be constant in your righteousness	*143*
Before the upper side of the twirl	*67*
Before Time began	*165*
Can one talk behind one's back	*79*
Closing a file drawer	*52*
Dear Saintly Dr Luke:	*135*
Deep—deep—deep within	*157*
deviled-eye	*167*
Did I write this? Say it?	*152*
Do you know what they	*122*
Don't tell me crocodilians head for the hills	*154*
Elegium Catullus/Corso	*25*
Every night of our youth	*25*
Forces of Nature that destroy man	*83*
From birth to '80 no one I knew died	*45*
Had you but loved the lesser love more	*90*
Head—bowed like a bull	*119*
He was 88 and had Alzheimer's	*65*
He was five kilometers	*162*
How can I convince you	*53*
How to lose fear	*82*
I am frighteningly lost in the present	*27*

I believe people are born	*49*
I can predict with 99 percent accuracy	*106*
I despise the intrusive telephone	*160*
I don't know how you could have been a different me	*140*
I dreamed what might have been my first dream	*73*
I feel like writing a beautiful poem	*71*
If I had strolled down the Via Sacra	*99*
I first entered the Tombs	*61*
If things of no import	*150*
I have a poem to tell.	*105*
I have grown up, haven't I?	*54*
I have near a decade of poems	*34*
I have nothing to say	*40*
I insisted on Beauty	*97*
I know where all the beauties are	*92*
I love you as I love my fear	*72*
I never really looked at my hands	*101*
IN THE END WAS THE WORD	*123*
In the first edition	*134*
In the middle 1950's	*123*
In time anger wrought of vengeance cools off and all is forgiven	*37*
Is love instinctive	*57*
It sneaks up on you	*35*
It was always old people told me	*56*
I was born 1930	*30*
I wish I had a bear for a friend	*120*
I've become a recluse	*32*
Just look how Nestor-smashed the skin	*108*
Make some friends	*132*
My ancestral home was the cave	*171*
MY KARMA RAN OVER MY DOGMA	*152*
My leadership ability	*98*
No, don't give me that	*89*

Not recognizing just the kind of person I was	*100*
O tell me nice man	*60*
Old age wills but once	*151*
Penguins and bears may tear up my sofa chairs	*44*
prepare for a dismissal of sorts	*64*
Reader	*111*
Reader, when poetry came to me	*137*
reluctant to sleep away this night	*38*
Say when my time is up	*76*
She poemed her words in circles	*131*
Space is in motion	*161*
Soul sickness devils the brain	*156*
Tell me not of time and places	*116*
The captain just went down	*141*
the dark night of the soul	*85*
The dark underside of saintliness	*117*
THE DAY MY FATHER DIED	*65*
The drums are beating	*164*
The illness of the winds	*102*
The mind goes round and round	*23*
the muse	*170*
the need is there	*168*
The old chemicals carried my labors, at times,	*43*
The possibilities	*118*
There is no time	*113*
There it was sitting across from me	*70*
There's one thing you'll never get from me	*47*
There were two times	*109*
The 3 of Ice	*146*
They know your condition	*149*
This brain a half century ago	*69*
This is an autobio	*29*
This is how it happened:	*103*

to write what in/or out of time	41
True, you have della Francesca, we have de Kooning;	112
Two funny things I worried about in life	78
Used to be the stamps of Egypt	114
weird traces of light like inverted shadows	26
What I don't know	59
What I want to know	42
when god is me	48
When in dream I flagellate	95
When something of power dies	96
When the one of the many that came	139
When the year 1 arrived for the descendants	86
Who can deny when a truth becomes redundant	74
Who taught me the song I sang?	159
Who was it	75
Would you have me believe he walks with spiked feet;	147
You 13 have your classical sources	88
You cannot replicate the soul	94
You never told me about Poe	80
YOU SAY BEAUTY, HOW FORTUNATE WE ARE: IT IS OLD OUR BEAUTY ALL OLD… DEATH FOLLOWS	*112*

Gregory Corso (1930-2001) was born in New York City's Greenwich Village. He was placed in numerous foster homes, and as a teenager served time in detention centers and prisons in New York and Vermont. His lifelong friendship with Allen Ginsberg began in 1951 with their meeting in a Greenwich Village bar, shortly after Corso's release from Clinton Correctional Facility. In 1954-55, Corso was based in Cambridge, Massachusetts, staying with friends from Harvard and Radcliffe colleges, and befriending Frank O'Hara and Bunny Lang at the Poet's Theater. His first book *The Vestal Lady on Brattle and Other Poems* was published there in 1955. As an original member of the Beat Generation along with Ginsberg, Herbert Huncke, William S. Burroughs and Jack Kerouac, Corso was a public figure and a poet of great popularity who published and read widely. In 1965 he was invited to teach at SUNY Buffalo but was dismissed upon arrival when he refused to sign a loyalty oath to the US Government. He lived a peripatetic life, dividing his time between New York, San Francisco, Paris, Rome, and Athens. A faculty member in poetics at the Naropa Institute in Boulder in the 1980s and 1990s, Corso died of prostate cancer in January 2001.

Raymond Foye is a writer, editor, publisher, and curator. He was a Director of Exhibitions and Publications at Gagosian Gallery from 1990-1995. He has edited titles for City Lights, New Directions, Black Sparrow Press, Alfred Knopf, Rizzoli's and Peterburg Press. With Francesco Clemente he edited and published Hanuman Books from 1985-1995, in India. He is the literary executor for the estates of John Wieners, James Schuyler, and Rene Ricard, and is a Consulting Editor at the *Brooklyn Rail*.

George Scrivani studied Latin and Greek at SUNY Buffalo, where he met Gregory Corso in 1970. For the next thirty years he served as Corso's secretary, editor, and translator (Italian and German). His translation of Alberto Savinio's *Departure of the Argonaut* was published by Peterburg Press in 1986, with illustrations by Francesco Clemente. Between 1985-1995 he worked in India as editor for Hanuman Books. He also pursued a professional medical career as a registered nurse.